THE TIMES
THE SUNDAY TIMES

Cover Ali smiles after defeating Archie Moore in 1962. Stanley Weston/Getty Images
Inside front Ali shadow-boxing at his mother's house in Louisville, Kentucky. Steve Schapiro/Getty Images
Below Ali celebrates after knocking out Cleveland Williams in 1966. Getty Images

Editor Tiffanie Darke
Design Ian 'Richy' Richardson, Valentina Verc
Sub-editor Warren Shore
Picture research Matthew Glynn, Lizzy Owen
Editorial research Jennifer Hahn

With thanks to Darren Smith, Louise Gordon, Elliott Florence, Brian Oliver, Lee Chilvers, Sue De Friend, Michael-John Jennings, Repro Services, Joanna Lodewyke, Tim Heming, Lisa Kjellsson, Samm Taylor, Annalee Mather

CONTRIBUTORS

HUGH McILVANNEY

The sports writer spent more one-to-one time with Ali than any other British reporter, having first met him in 1963

MICHAEL PARKINSON

A British TV institution, the chat-show host interviewed the American on four memorable occasions

CHRIS SMITH

The Sunday Times photographer travelled the world taking classic pictures of Ali both in and out of the ring

NEIL ALLEN

As Olympic Games and boxing correspondent for The Times, he covered the fighter's entire career

MATTHEW SYED

An Olympian like Ali, he left behind table tennis to become an award-winning journalist

RON LEWIS

The boxing and athletics correspondent for The Times compiled our guide to Ali's fights

ALI
THE DEFINITIVE GUIDE

'ALI WAS THE POSSESSOR OF UTTERLY SPECIAL GIFTS'

The champion of champions was an unforgettable presence in the ring and outside it, writes **Hugh McIlvanney**, who spent many hours in his company

Right

Ali goads Joe Frazier in 1974, telling his great rival that he will see an ugly man if he looks into a car's wing mirror

t is pretty much incontestable that at the height of his fame as the most compelling figure in the history of sport, and self-appointed master of ceremonies to mankind, Muhammad Ali was the most widely recognised human being on the planet. No contemporary political figure, however influential or notorious, impinged on the consciousness of so many people. Nor did the most celebrated film stars or entertainers. When the Beatles met up with him on their tour of America early in 1964, he was still two or three weeks away from the sensational defeat of Sonny Liston that made him undisputed heavyweight champion of the world barely a month after his 22nd birthday. Yet even then John, Paul, Ringo and George accepted happily enough that while they were in his company they would be the supporting act.

The legitimising platform for his capacity to enthral was always the prodigious scale of the athletic gifts that enabled him to become the only boxer who has ever reigned three times as the master of the heavyweights, a distinction whose worth is unimaginable now that the proliferation of sanctioning bodies has fractured the world title beyond recognition. Ali would not have been able to behave as if addressing the earth's masses from a celestial podium had he not brought a sense of the epic to the blood-and-snot business transacted inside the ropes.

His feats there provided the original and sustained validation of his claim on our attention, from the toppling of two men who had assumed the fearsomeness of ogres, Liston and George Foreman, to his dramatic trilogy of confrontations with his truest and most respected adversary, Joe Frazier. But his appeal owed at least as much to the effect of a beautiful and magnetising physical presence and an essentially unsophisticated but uniquely captivating personality, a central element of which was a genius for the comic so engaging that he was capable of spreading not just laughter but joy.

Like his joking, the entire impact of his life owed much to its timing. He erupted among us when the reach of electronic media was widening exponentially and television identified him as demanding tireless coverage. His iconoclasm, too, as a sportsman and as a social force, gained in authority from having a helpful historical context. The 1960s was a period when rebelliousness was rife in many societies and he was adopted as a symbol of its best aspirations. But the circumstances of the age don't begin to explain the miracles of popularity and relevance he wrought. Future historians, when assessing the Ali phenomenon, may find themselves concerned less with the self-transcending power of sporting greatness than with the mysterious alchemy by which he generated in a huge swathe of humanity not so much affection and approval as a feeling that permits no definition other than love.

By no means everything he did contributed to the accumulation of that near-universal warmth towards him. Even the defiance of white society's oppressive attitudes that earned him the status of a standard-bearer for black pride might have been considered tainted when he showered taunts and cruel Uncle Tom insults on ring opponents with much rawer experience of colour prejudice than he ever had. And listeners did not have to be redneck bigots to be appalled and angered by the deranged virulence of the racist diatribes he spouted when preaching the doctrines that constituted the creed of the Nation of Islam while

Elijah Muhammad, aka the Messenger, was its leader. Yet Ali was never remotely convincing as a hater and his admirers didn't feel they were being naive in claiming to recognise, beyond what they saw as outrageous role-playing, the lovable core of an intrinsically good man. They remained sure it was not merely natural but right to be enraptured by him.

The light that dazzled so irresistibly was doused long ago. For more than 30 years the man who persuaded us to regard him as The Greatest had been imprisoned in the twilit existence decreed by an inexorably engulfing infirmity, a merciless decline directly caused by absorbing too many punches to the head. When his feet were dancing and his gloved hands were achieving a swiftness and fluency never seen from a man of his size before or since, when he revelled in acting out and verbalising his own Superman scripts,

untold numbers seemed to be mesmerised into imagining the violence they witnessed was occurring in some kind of comic-strip dimension where their hero wasn't subject to the harsh consequences of his trade. But Superman was suffering brain damage.

Years prior to his retirement in 1981 there were unmistakable portents of the problems ahead, of the Parkinson's syndrome (not Parkinson's disease but a condition with similar symptoms attributed in his case to physical trauma of the brain stem) that would freeze his once vibrant features into an expressionless mask, make his arms tremble uncontrollably, bring a leaden ponderousness to his walk and reduce the voice that riveted his global audience to a blurred whisper often indecipherable at a distance of a couple of feet. Eventually the noisiest of athletes was trapped in virtual silence, generally restricted to communicating the mischief still active in

his brain through sign language — as when, while at the White House in 2005 to receive the Presidential Medal of Freedom, he responded to George W Bush's mock offer to trade punches by putting a shaky right index finger to his temple and twirling it.

Ali was anything but the darling of his government on the previous occasion when he could be said to have fronted up to the Commander-in-Chief, by refusing to be drafted into the US army in 1967. He cited his religious beliefs but the quotes forever connected with his stance present a plainer justification: "I ain't got no quarrel with them Viet Cong" and the appropriation of the black activist Stokely Carmichael's line, "No Viet Cong ever called me nigger". The five-year jail sentence handed down for refusing the draft hung over him as a genuine threat until in 1971 the Supreme Court swung from 5-3 in favour of affirming his conviction to 8-0 for overturning it.

His admirers were sure it was not merely natural but right to be enraptured by him

He did have to endure the incarceration of his talent and his earning power. American boxing authorities reacted with vindictive alacrity to his declaration that he wouldn't serve in the army, ruling he was no longer champion and ensuring that no US state would license him to fight. With his passport revoked, he faced an exile from the ring whose cost was certain to be physical as well as financial. It was to last three and a half years and when he returned to action in October 1970 the leg speed that had been such a vital component of his extravagantly idiosyncratic fighting style was largely a memory, and he had to rely increasingly on his freakish ability to withstand head punches. No boxer I ever saw did that more amazingly than Ali but the awe his resilience evoked was always accompanied by deep dread of its implications for his health.

However, long before the misgivings closed in on our appreciation of him with the full force of guilt, he had used the second phase of his career to make irrefutable the case for acknowledging that, in the entire annals of sport, he was an unparalleled wonder. That span contained the dramas with Frazier and Foreman, the second and third winning of the heavyweight title, countless demonstrations that he could be as hypnotically theatrical outside the ring as he was in it — and, above all, the maturing of the world's love affair with the story begun in the maternity ward of Louisville General Hospital in Kentucky on January 17, 1942. At birth Ali, who would stand 6ft 3in and have an ideal weight of a few pounds over 15st in his prime, was an unspectacular 6lb 7oz but it's recorded that the size of his head meant doctors had to use forceps to ease him from his mother's womb. The mark left on his right cheek would seldom be noticed amid the striking handsomeness his face developed through his teenage years.

His parents could scarcely have presented more of a contrast. His mother had been Odessa Lee Grady (one of her grandfathers, Abe Grady, was from Ireland) when she married Cassius Marcellus Clay, whose resonant name was bestowed on him in honour of the 19th-century Kentucky landowner, politician and abolitionist who had freed his grandfather from slavery. She was a sweet-natured churchgoer. Her choice of husband was good-looking, small and athletically trim, but he was also a roguish and volatile womaniser with a taste for whisky and an even bigger enthusiasm for fantasising exotic identities for himself.

Cassius Sr could be a serious menace and on three occasions Odessa had to summon the police to protect her from him. Though such happenings must have cast a shadow over the early lives of Cassius Jr and his year-younger brother Rudolph Arnett/Valentino Clay, their childhoods seem to

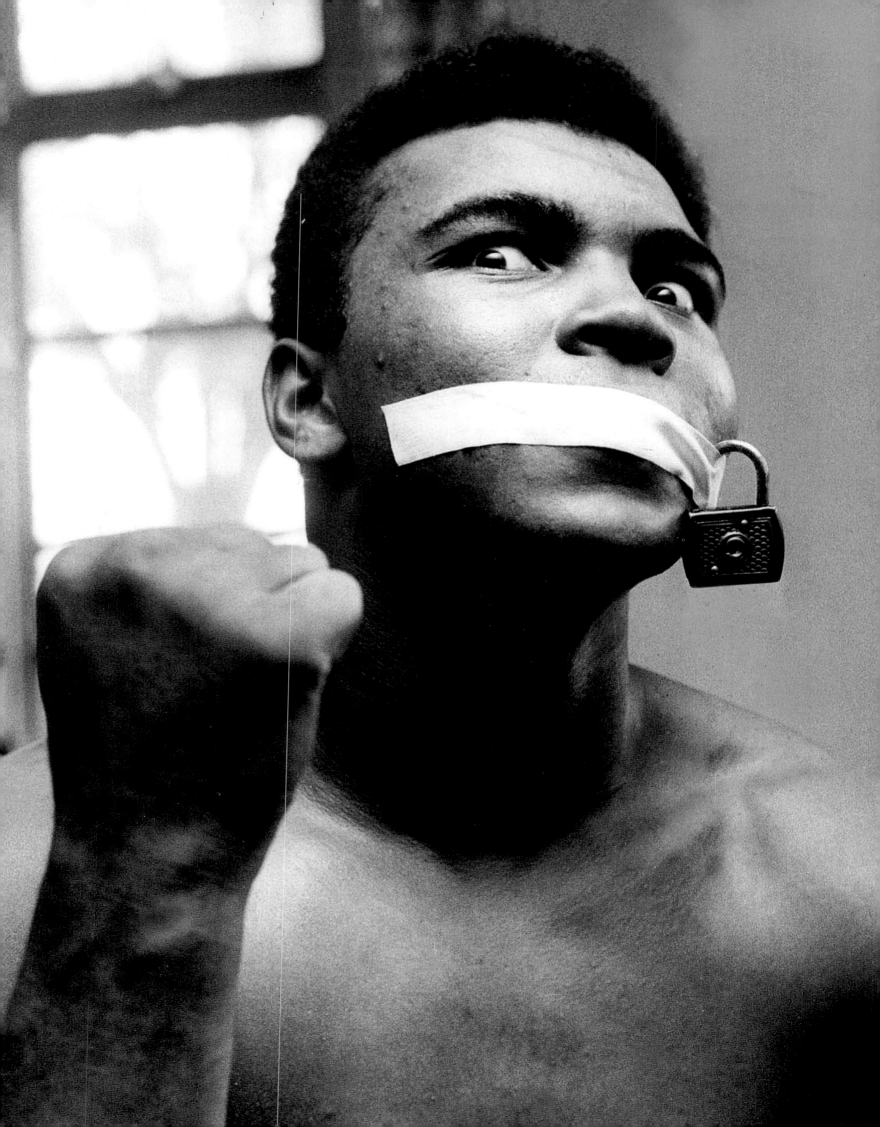

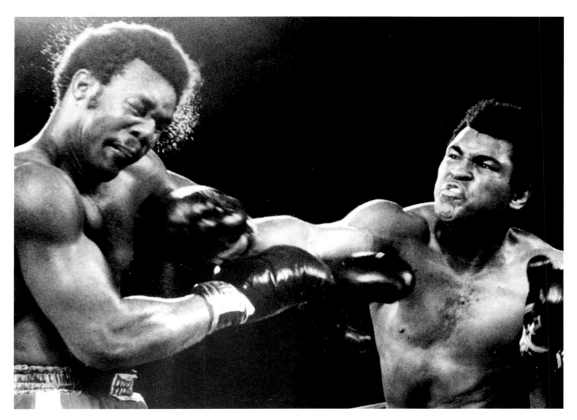

George Foreman recoils from a brutal right-hander at 1974's Rumble in the Jungle

have been mainly happy enough and the family were more comfortable economically than most of those around them in their black neighbourhood of Louisville.

Before he met his childhood trainer Joe Martin, Cassius Jr was briefly tutored by Fred Stoner, a black boxing trainer with professional associations. But there is no evidence that either teacher influenced his ideas about how he should perform in the ring. Nobody ever did much of that.

He was an inspired autodidact whose techniques would be shaped by an impregnable awareness that he was the possessor of utterly special gifts: extraordinary speed in his hands and feet; preternaturally quick reflexes; the mental sharpness to read and frustrate or, preferably, exploit an opponent's intentions; and the diamond nerve to keep faith with those assets when beset by extreme hazard. By the time a glittering amateur career was climaxed with the light-heavyweight gold medal at the 1960 Olympics, he had made highly personalised unorthodoxies the fundamentals of his ring arsenal.

He did not block, smother or duck threatening punches, opting instead to trust those divine reflexes and the flexibility of his torso to let him twist and lean fractionally out of range of danger, often with his arms dangling by his sides. He seldom set himself to punch with maximum leverage, content to deliver on the move, usually while circling his opponent. Fighting on the inside had no part in his method and his blows were aimed almost exclusively at the head. The harshest judges couldn't

withhold admiration of his exceptional speed and agility, and they had particular praise for the accuracy and suddenness of his left jab, but they felt there was something amateurish about his work in the ring. They weren't wrong, and the elements of his style that caused them to wince were not temporary. Much of what he did in the glory years ahead would be in violation of hallowed tenets of the professional ring. But he made it hard to distinguish between amateurishness and creative originality, and his immunity to convention helped him to expand the tactical inventiveness in which he took huge pride. He rightly believed he understood his fighting equipment better than anybody else.

The 18-year-old Cassius Clay was launched into professionalism under the auspices of the Louisville Sponsoring Group, a collection of wealthy white men whose reasons for investing in him ranged from the straightforwardly commercial to a more idealistic concern for the welfare of a local hero. Their contract with him would last until the autumn of 1966 when, with the draft controversy swirling around him and his commitment to the Nation of Islam established as the central influence on his life, the management of his career was taken over by one of Eijah Muhammad's sons, Herbert Muhammad.

Herbert couldn't complain about what he got out of a deal that never brought him less than a third of Ali's income from boxing and other activities. With Herbert, worldliness always outweighed ideology when it came to protecting his interests, which was why

Keeping the outspoken Ali quiet was a rare achievement

A glittering amateur career climaxed in Rome

from the moment he became Ali's manager he had never shown any inclination to question the wisdom of the Louisville Sponsoring Group in having appointed the Italian-American Angelo Dundee as the prodigy's trainer.

At that stage nearly every name on the list of victims was notable for being unnotable (Archie Moore was a glorious exception but he was in his late forties) and in disposing of them Ali hadn't always been coruscating. There was still a widespread readiness to suspect that his brash volubility and the bellowed proclamations of how incomparable he was would far overreach anything he did in the ring.

Dick Sadler, a top-rank trainer who would much later be in George Foreman's corner for the Rumble in the Jungle, tells in Thomas Hauser's impressive oral biography, Muhammad Ali: His Life and Times, of a train journey he made from California to Texas with the Cassius Clay who had one pro win to his credit. Sadler recalls: "The kid would be standing shouting out of the carriage, 'I am the greatest, I am the greatest'. He'd shout this at the passing cars and sheep and fields and stuff."

He was anything but the favourite in February 1964 when he went through the ropes in Miami to challenge for Liston's heavyweight title. His sensational victory over Liston was the big breakthrough on the road to acceptance as The Greatest. And if the action in the ring had demanded headlines, the press conferences held on the next two days produced stories with far wider implications. They confirmed something already close to being common knowledge: the new heavyweight champion was a member of the Nation of Islam, or the Black Muslims as the bulk of the press chose to call the organisation led by Elijah Muhammad. Cassius Clay was to be reincarnated as Muhammad Ali.

Nobody could then, or should now, doubt the sincerity of a conversion that instantly brought down on him the vitriolic hostility of the vast majority of white Americans and the troubled disapproval of many blacks. White sports writers were infuriated by his contempt for their idea of how a black champion should conduct himself, which meant adhering to the example of the inveterately amenable Joe Louis, the man one of the convert's fiercest critics, Jimmy

Cannon, had described as "a credit to his race — the human race".

It wasn't surprising that, as he sought spiritual moorings, somebody characterised by Ebony magazine in 1963 as "a blast furnace of racial pride" would be drawn to the Nation of Islam. His commitment to it would assail him with confusions, dangers and moral questions he frequently failed to answer creditably. It brought change to every area of his life. As early as 1965, the year when his second defeat of Liston solidified his position as heavyweight champion, proof of how intimate the influence of the Muslims could be came with the ending of Ali's first marriage.

Herbert Muhammad had introduced him to Sonji Roi, a beautiful 23-year-old mother who worked as a cocktail waitress and photographer's model. Six weeks later they were married, in August 1964, but Sonji was neither a Muslim nor submissive to the Nation's inhibiting rules and their relationship was over by the following summer and severed by divorce in January 1966. Ali's second wife, Belinda, was 17 on her wedding day in 1967, a strong-natured Muslim girl who was to bear him four children. She tolerated her husband's numerous adulteries and when Veronica Porsche started appearing frequently at Ali's side Belinda saw her as "just another one of the bunch". But when Ali, in the Philippines for the 1975 Thrilla in Manila and meeting the presidential couple, Ferdinand and Imelda Marcos, presented Veronica as his wife, Belinda flew from Chicago for a showdown. Its storminess rearranged the furniture in a hotel bedroom and left their marriage in ruins.

Within 24 hours Belinda was flying home, knowing Ali had exchanged her for Veronica, although it would be a year and a half before he and his new woman completed the matrimonial formalities. Veronica seemed more of a glamorous adjunct to Ali than a caring partner or a benign presence and few were surprised when, with his boxing career long gone and his health rapidly declining, there was a divorce in 1986 that provided her with an enormously generous settlement. By then another woman — one 14 years his junior who, as a child, had hero-worshipped him when he visited the home of her parents, neighbours of the Clays — had resurfaced in his life as a supportive influence, and in November 1986 Yolanda (Lonnie) Williams became his fourth wife. They had been together ever since and had an adopted son. Ali fathered eight children, seven daughters (two out of wedlock) and a son.

Lonnie was in primary school when Ali was in his prime as an athlete, which he reached in the years between his double humiliation of Liston and the ban imposed for the refusal to be drafted. Some of his eight defences of the heavyweight

title in that period invited opprobrium rather than praise. That was especially true of his taunting prolongation of the suffering of two outclassed challengers — Floyd Patterson, who had poured acid condemnation on the Muslims, and Ernie Terrell, who called him Clay instead of Ali. But no amount of resentment of how he used his skills could blind anyone to the simple truth that his talent had soared to a standard the heavyweight division had never seen previously and was never likely to see again. That was encapsulated in the greatest exhibition of boxing virtuosity he ever produced, the three rounds in which he dazzled and devastated Cleveland Williams on November 14, 1966, in Houston. Ali moved with the speed of a welterweight that night and his punching was a miraculous blend of timing, precision and punishing force. Opinions on where he stands in the pantheon of heavyweight champions should be based on how he was then.

By the spring of 1967, Ali was an outcast from boxing. He had originally failed the

An early-morning training run through Hyde Park in London, 1963

army's mental tests in 1964, scoring 16 against a pass mark of 30. He was classified 1-Y and unfit for service. But two years later, with the Vietnam War expanding, the mental-aptitude percentile required by the military was lowered from 30 to 15, and Ali was eligible for the draft.

The artist in Ali had markedly reduced capacity for self-expression in the ring when he was permitted to box again in 1970. It was after his return to action that covering his dramas provided the highlight experiences of my decades as a sports writer. Not least because they include his three-part series with Frazier and the blockbuster with Foreman. There, also, are echoes of the sadness stirred in me and millions of others by the ineluctable erosion of his powers and the signs that his increasing exposure to heavy punishment was building up health problems for him. However, medical advice had never stood much chance against the combination of pressures pushing Ali in the opposite direction.

He had been given a lot of help in disposing

> His talent soared to a standard the heavyweight division had never seen

of the $40m in purses he was estimated to have collected to that point. The need for money and an addiction to attention guaranteed that Ali would resist retirement until every possibility of postponing it was beaten out of his skull. It was in 1984, nearly three years after his final misery in the ring, that Ali checked into the Columbia-Presbyterian Medical Centre in New York. He did not have Parkinson's disease but Parkinsonism or Parkinson's syndrome. All agreed the source of his afflictions was boxing. "If Muhammad hadn't been a professional fighter, none of these problems would have occurred," said Dr Dennis Cope, who treated him regularly.

Another transformation of his life awaited at the opening ceremony of the 1996 Olympics in Atlanta. There were people beside me in the stadium, and no doubt millions in the worldwide television audience, who thought it was unforgivably exploitative, almost sadistic, to ask him to take the Olympic Torch in his violently shaking hands and struggle with agonising slowness to where he could light the flame that would burn through the Games. But there were infinitely more of us who were unbearably moved by the white-clad figure we couldn't resist regarding as an embodiment of tragedy and triumph. For a majority of Americans, the moment swept away the ambiguities of feeling that had lingered around all the contradictions of Ali's past, and only love was left.

There remains a conviction that he never ceased to deserve this assessment from Gerald Early, a professor at Washington University in St Louis, who provides a black intellectual's perspective: "Like all great heroes he showed us the enormous possibility of the true meaning, the incendiary poetics, of actual self-determination." Through most of his adult life Ali delighted in making handkerchiefs disappear, in trying to persuade watchers he was levitating and in performing other feats from the amateur magician's repertoire. But the world knew that the most magical trick of all was himself.

Left
The doting father relaxes with his daughters Laila, left, and Hana in 1978

Left
Addressing the Illinois State Athletic Commission in 1966 over his 'unpatriotic' remarks

THE RING MASTER: A TRIUMPH OF TALENT AND TECHNIQUE

RON LEWIS

There had never been a heavyweight like Muhammad Ali. Quick, loose-limbed and always moving, he used his speed as much for defence as attack. He changed boxing as much through his talent and technique as through his personality.

The blueprint for a top-class heavyweight usually involved a good jab and plenty of power. Being light on your feet was not normally a requirement. Ali was as fast going forward as backwards, he could lean in and out of range, never setting a still target. He was better at slipping punches than blocking them.

When most people think of his footwork, they recall the Ali Shuffle. What he did within range was always more impressive. Ali seldom moved in straight lines, he could slip punches inside and outside, but because his footwork was so good, he could counter brilliantly, switching defence to attack in a split-second.

The speed of the young Cassius Clay was his main asset. After winning the world heavyweight title, Ali learned to sit down on his punches better, to hold his feet while punching. But a changed Ali returned from his three-year ban, lacking the hand speed and the same reflexes. After losing to Joe Frazier and Ken Norton, he became technically shrewder. He continued to slow after his third fight against Frazier and in the final part of his career lacked the engine to fight a full 15 rounds.

At his best, Ali's power came from speed and timing. His balance was so impressive, allowing him to throw hard shots with both hands or as part of one movement after slipping a punch. He put together five- or six-punch combinations, almost unheard of from a heavyweight before or since.

EARLY YEARS

1942-1960

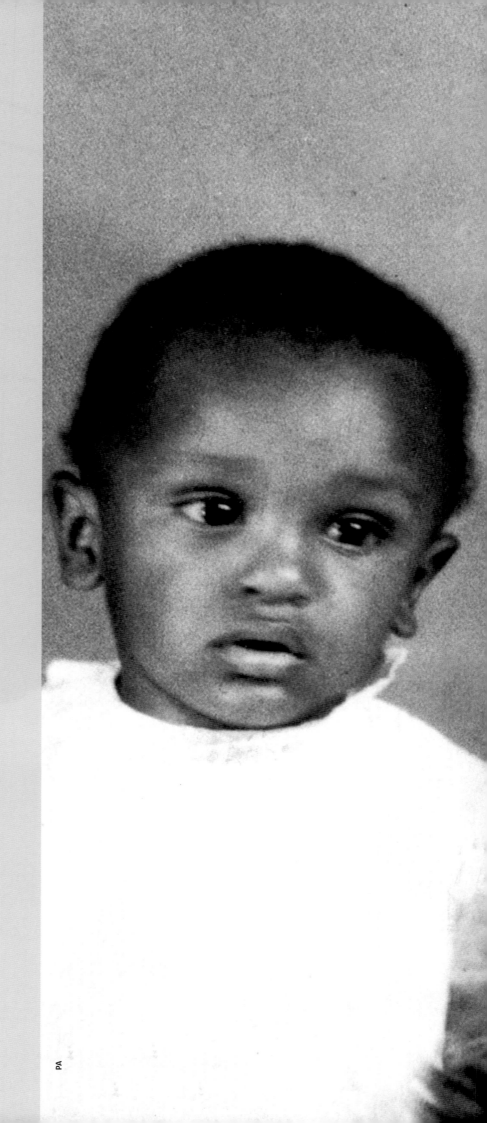

He was in the bed at six months and hit me in the mouth when he stretched. It loosened my front tooth and affected my other front tooth. I had to have both pulled out. I always say his first knockout punch was in my mouth

PA

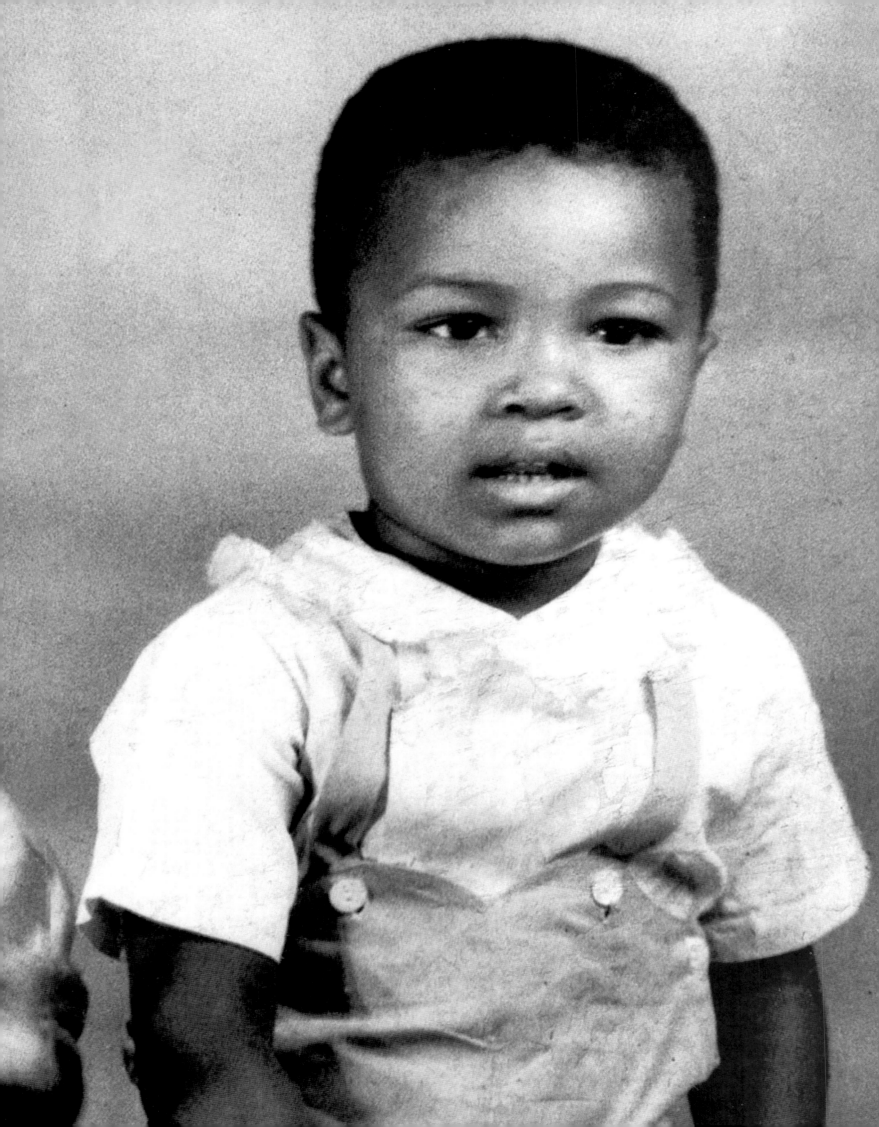

'I WANT TO BE A BOXER'

Muhammad Ali recalls how the sight of a neighbourhood gym made a big impression on him as a popcorn-munching 12-year-old

Across the street from Nazareth College is Columbia Gym, where I first started boxing but not where I learned the science of it. The story that my boxing career began because my bike was stolen is a true one, as far as it goes. But that was only a part of it. I was 12 years old, and me and Johnny Willis, my closest buddy, had been out riding around on our bikes until the rain got too heavy. We were looking for something else to do when Johnny suddenly remembered seeing an ad for a black business exhibition at Columbia Auditorium on 4th and York. The auditorium is a big recreational centre, with a boxing gym and a bowling alley. Every year the black people in the city hold a big bazaar, the Louisville Home Show, at the Columbia Gym.

At first I didn't want to go to the Home Show but when we read the leaflet we saw that there would be free popcorn, free hot dogs and free candy. Besides, my father had bought me a new bike for Christmas, a Schwinn with red lights and chrome trim, and I wanted to show it off.

At the show we focused in on the food, and we hung around eating until seven o'clock, when everybody was leaving. The rain was still coming down heavy as we left, so it took a while for us to notice that my bicycle was gone. Angry and frightened of what my father would do, we ran up and down the streets, asking about the bike. Someone told us to go downstairs to the Columbia Gym: "There's a policeman, Joe Elsby Martin, down there in the recreation centre. Go and see him."

I ran downstairs, crying, but the sights and sounds and the smell of the boxing gym excited me so much that I almost forgot about the bike. There were about ten boxers in the gym, some hitting the speed bag, some in the ring, sparring, some jumping rope. I stood there, smelling the sweat and rubbing alcohol, and a feeling of awe came over me. One slim boy shadow-boxing in the ring was throwing punches almost too

When I stood in that gym, smelling the sweat, a feeling of awe came over me

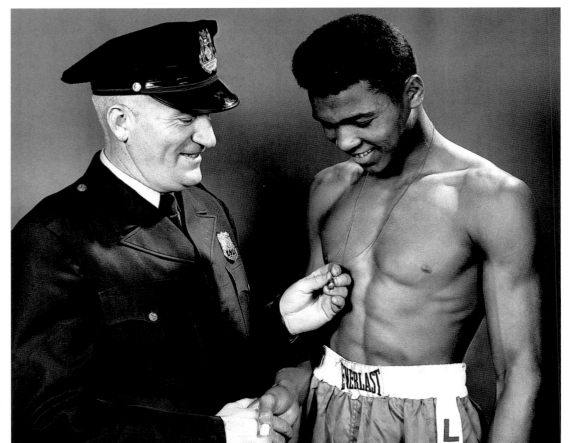

POPPERFOTO/PICTORIAL PRESS/ALAMY/SIPA USA/PA

fast for my eyes to follow. "You'll have to give me a report," Martin said calmly, and wrote down what I told him. Then, as I was about to go, he tapped me on the shoulder. "By the way, we got boxing every night, Monday through Friday, from six to eight. Here's an application in case you want to join the gym."

I was about 112lb, skinny, and I'd never had on a pair of boxing gloves. I folded up the paper and stuck it in my pocket, thinking it was a poor thing to take home instead of my bike.

Later I was home looking at a TV show, an amateur boxing show, and there was the face of Joe Martin, working in the corner with one of his boys.

I nudged my mother. "That's the man I told about the bicycle. He wants me to come and box. Where's that application?"

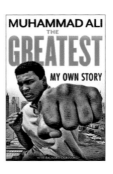

MUHAMMAD ALI
THE
GREATEST
MY OWN STORY

Extracted from The Greatest: My Own Story by Muhammad Ali with Richard Durham (Graymalkin Media)

Left
Boxing commentators were caught by surprise when they saw at close quarters the style and punching power of American newcomer Cassius Clay at the Rome Olympics

Right
Clay stands on the Palazzo dello Sport podium to receive his gold medal after defeating the Polish fighter Zbigniew Pietrzykowski

Below
In training for the Games, at which he was 18 years of age

STRIKING OLYMPIC GOLD

Cassius Clay was a shy teenager when he fought at the Rome Games in 1960. He returned as a champion to 'the best country in the world'. By **Neil Allen**

We went as far back as the Rome Olympics of 1960 where the then Cassius Marcellus Clay won the lightheavyweight gold medal. At those Games, the second of six I covered for *The Times*, the 18-year-old Clay, from Louisville, Kentucky, was wide-eyed, shy and so afraid of flying ("he insisted you could get to Rome from the States by train", a contemporary said) that he sat on a private parachute all the way across the Atlantic.

My first ringside view of "the most" saw him have some trouble in his Olympic semi-final against the experienced Australian Tony Madigan. For the final against the tongue-twisting Zbigniew Pietrzykowski, Poland's triple European amateur champion, young Cassius had to be more than "mean and hungry".

Tongue in cheek for his first international press conference, he told us: "I'm gonna hit that Pole with two fast jabs, a right cross and a left hook. If he's still standing after that, and the ref ain't holding him up, then . . . I run."

In Rome's splendid Palazzo dello Sport, the experienced Pietrzykowski, a superb exponent of the eastern European state-backed amateur style, held the centre of the ring like a gladiator. He clearly had the best of the first round against the retreating youngster and most of the second except that, just before the bell, the inexperienced American landed four thudding right hands. By the end of the third the Pole was reeling, bleeding and beaten.

At the post-fight interview, a Soviet reporter predictably asked the young black American how he would cope with racism when he returned home. "We got qualified people working on that," was the reply from the gold medal-winner, "but the US is the best country in the world."

The teenager from the black equivalent of the American middle class added carefully: "It's hard sometimes to get something to eat but I ain't fighting alligators and living in a mud hut."

I choose to remember him as the No 1 man of all my years in writing about sport, whose bubbling, mischievous, occasionally spiteful mind could transform a press conference just as, in his prime, he could turn the hardest game into a balletic demonstration of speed and skill.

CAREER TAKEOFF

1960-1964

I'm not the greatest, I'm the double greatest. Not only do I knock 'em out, I pick the round. I'm the boldest, the prettiest, the most superior, most scientific, most skilfullest fighter in the ring today

AFTER DEFEATING HENRY COOPER AT
WEMBLEY STADIUM IN 1963

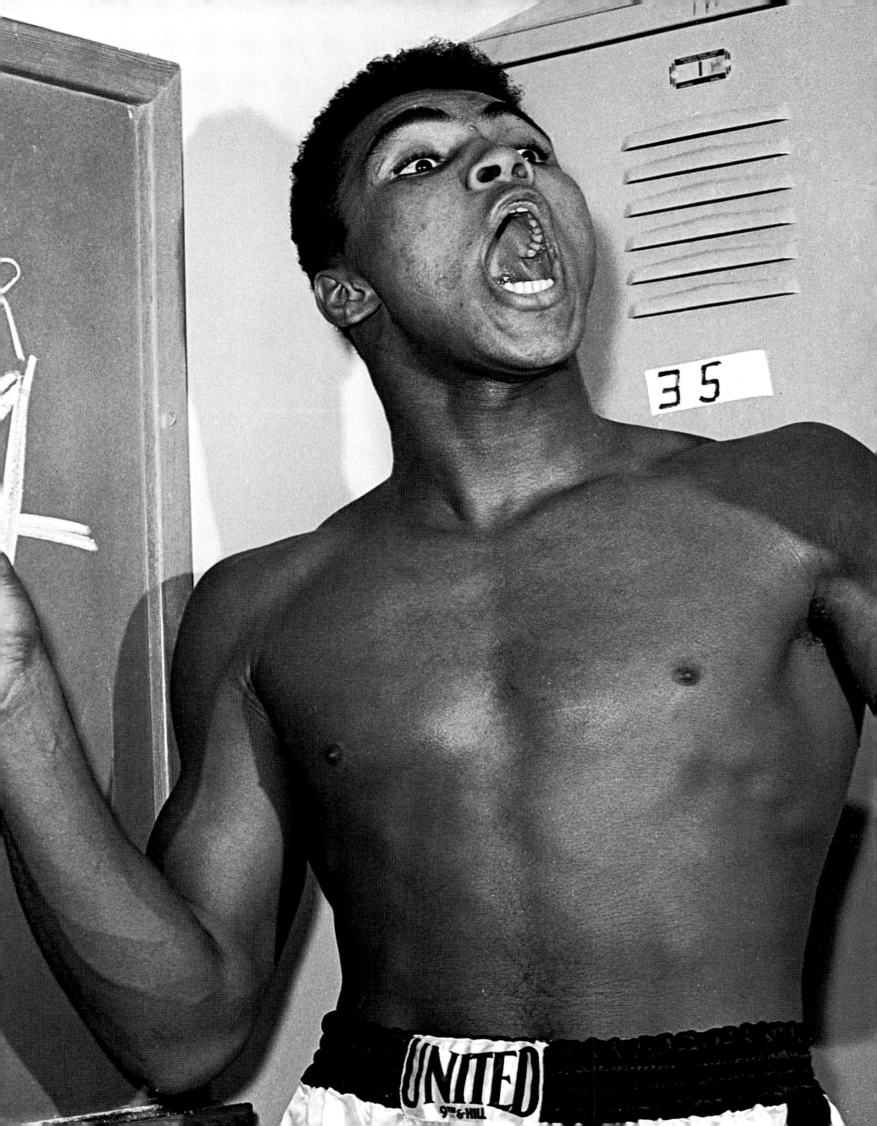

'He beamed at Cassius as if he were an oil well who had just turned up in his backyard'

The Greatest caused a stir wherever he went and that was certainly the case when he fought Henry Cooper, writes Neil Allen

The one time I saw the motormouth shut tight was in July 1963 when Clay came to London to box Britain's popular Henry Cooper in the first of their two bouts. Clay had stripped right down for an official pre-fight medical examination when the British Boxing Board's chairman, Jack Onslow Fane, with all the confidence of an Old Etonian, remarked: "My dear Mr Cassius, I must say you have the most magnificent a***."

Just a couple of nights later the Clay posterior was bouncing on the Wembley canvas only inches away from my front-row seat after he had been dropped at the end of the fourth round by a cracking Cooper left hook while, sjust behind, Richard Burton and Elizabeth Taylor were screaming the British hero on.

Incidentally, exact BBC radio recordings of the sound of the bell to end the fourth round, and then to start the fifth, disprove the legend that Clay's astute, influential trainer Angelo Dundee had gained his man vital recovery time by widening a tear in one of his gloves. The time gained was definitely less than ten seconds.

FROM THE ARCHIVES

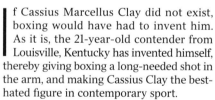

A REAL LIVE WIRE

The fighter was playing up to the audience when David Leitch met him in London on June 2, 1963

If Cassius Marcellus Clay did not exist, boxing would have had to invent him. As it is, the 21-year-old contender from Louisville, Kentucky has invented himself, thereby giving boxing a long-needed shot in the arm, and making Cassius Clay the best-hated figure in contemporary sport.

Last week in the gymnasium near the White City, where he is doing some perfunctory training for his Wembley fight, Cassius treated me to the silly routine that has made him famous. "Say, who is this bum Cooper? He must fall in five ... I'll hit him so fast he'll think he's surrounded and London will be jarred, man ..." On and on it went, all delivered in a soft, unconvincing voice as though he were repeating a boring lesson tediously committed to memory.

"Yeah, when he gets in that ring he'll think he's Gordon Cooper, 22 times in orbit..." Cassius went on talking like a tap dripping. Inconspicuous among the crowd of helpers, Rudolf Valentino Clay, the heavyweight's brother and sparring partner who plans to turn pro himself in August watched the act with a faint air of embarrassment. Had Cassius always been so conceited?

Above

Leaping for joy, Ali, then Cassius Clay, jumps over a fence in Hyde Park the day after beating Henry Cooper

Left

Ali wears a policeman's helmet as he mixes with fans in London in 1980

WHAT IT FELT LIKE TO KNOCK DOWN THE GREATEST

HENRY COOPER

I caught Ali with a clean left hook in the fourth round, one of the best I'd ever thrown. As the punch connected, I could see that he was gone. In boxing, the eyes tell you everything and I could see the whites of his.

It was a shame he wasn't in the centre of the ring because as he went down, the ropes broke his fall. Then the bell came to his rescue.

I remember thinking how lucky the bell was for him because when I had people in trouble in those days, I always finished them off.

But I didn't have the chance because his trainer, Angelo Dundee, was a shrewd man and stuck his nails into Ali's glove to rip it and cause a delay.

I hadn't been surprised that he went down. I'd fancied my chances because I suspected that he wouldn't like my style. He was flash, but people forget he had great heart in the ring.

Ali had since said that I hit him so hard that when he hit the ground, his relations could feel it reverberating in Africa.

ALI RECOVERED TO WIN BY TKO AGAINST COOPER IN THE FIFTH ROUND

"I guess he got going after the Rome Olympics, when he turned pro. You could say one Cassius in the family is enough." He went on looking patiently at his brother who started to talk sense for the first time. "I turned pro cos medals and trophies and knives and forks aren't good American dollars. Then I started predicting — Moore will fall in four. I said, Cassius, it's a long hard road ahead and this way you'll get twice as much notice as other contenders. Wasn't I right? They pay to see me fall."

Had Cassius dreamt it all up or had a bright publicity man had the idea? "No, no, no it was me, I thought of predicting. I'm the captain on this ship: I say stay cool, this ship's not gonna sink while I'm here."

Did Cassius have views on integration? A slight murmur of consternation came from Rudolf and Cassius twisted his face as though Sonny Liston had hit him. "Twice a day people ask me to take part in this. I can't. I'm no leader, I never went near college. Integration's gotta come, but somebody's gotta die first and I don't want poison in my food. If a white man don't want me then I don't wanna mix. I'll stay with my own." Cassius may not be a scholar but it took brains to see his route to the top, to realise that crowds will pay to see the high-wire artists because there is always a chance he will fall. He has a soft, untouched face, not the face of a man who finds it easy to be hated or be alone on the high-wire.

When the conversation turned to money he cheered up. "Cassius filled the Garden, $280,000 cash at the door, $560,000 from closed circuit TV. Hey, how much at Wembley?" Jack Solomons [the promoter] wasn't saying, but he beamed at Cassius as though he were an oil well that had just appeared in the backyard.

"Joe Louis was a nice guy, but where did it get him?" asked Cassius. "In debt to the government, that's where. I don't wanna be a silent fighter in an empty arena." And he started again about what he was going to do to Cooper.

Right

Henry Cooper floors Cassius Clay with a left hook in the fourth round of their fight at Wembley on June 18, 1963

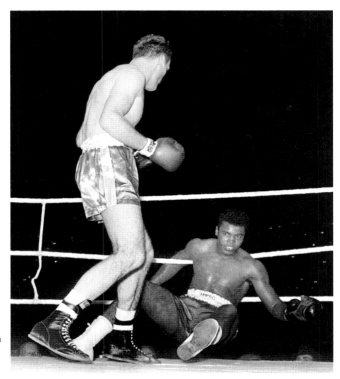

THE BEST SEAT IN THE HOUSE

Trainer Angelo Dundee told **Brian Doogan** about his unforgettable years in Ali's corner — and the tricks of his trade at ringside

Angelo Dundee's introduction to Cassius Clay came unexpectedly on the afternoon of February 19, 1957, at the Sheraton Hotel in Louisville, Kentucky, where he was staying with the fighter Willie Pastrano.

"The phone rang in my room. I picked it up and what I can only describe as a great rush of words rained down on my ear: 'My name is Cassius Marcellus Clay and I am the Golden Gloves champion of Louisville, the Golden Gloves champion of Atlanta, the Golden Gloves champion of Seattle, I am going to Rome to win the Olympic Games gold medal for America and one day I will be heavyweight champion of the world.' My God. the kid could talk even then.

"He rambled on some more and then he said, 'Mr Dundee, I'm downstairs with my brother and we'd like to come up to speak to you and Mr Pastrano.' I said to the kid to come up to the room and we'd give him and his brother five minutes."

Below

Dundee, right, takes care of his man during the 1966 bout with Karl Mildenberger

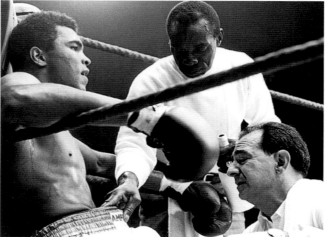

More than three hours later they were still talking and the Louisville Lip was driving the conversation, Dundee recalled. "He was a student of boxing and wanted to know every facet of the business. 'What do your fighters eat? How many miles do they run? Mr Pastrano, what was your toughest fight?' The inquisition was endless. He had a thirst for information and he never lost this. When the kid left the room, finally, I had a big smile on my face and so did Willie. Neither of us had ever come across anyone like him."

For more than 50 years, Dundee remained a part of Ali's life, taking over his training after his first professional fight in October 1960 against Tunney Hunsaker. "People talk about the great talent the kid had, the way he was athletically gifted and how he was blessed with speed, all of which is true," Dundee told me at his home outside Tampa, Florida, in 2007. "He was a phenomenal specimen, a unique athlete. He loved to fight and he loved to train. A lot of fighters don't like to train. It's boring but he made it fun, alive. He was a joy."

After completing his road work in the morning he would run from his hotel in Miami across the MacArthur Causeway to the Fifth Street Gym. At that time "people of colour" were not permitted by law to be in Miami Beach between sunset and sunrise, so when he was pulled over by police in semi-darkness one morning, wearing his running gear, Dundee had to vouch for him.

"That's Cassius doing his road work," he told the cops. "You're going to be seeing a lot of him around here."

Clay's record was 18-0 when he went to London in 1963 to box Henry Cooper. "I spent time in England when I was in the military and I developed a great love for the English. They used to invite you to dinner when they didn't have any food, this is how hospitable they were, so I thought they would love Cassius," said Dundee. "I was wrong. The second time he went over, which would have been after he had won the title from Sonny Liston, it was crazy. We couldn't walk outside because he was mobbed wherever he went. We used to go to a restaurant in London and one night we couldn't move our car away because some people in the crowd had taken the air out of the tyres. Muhammad just got out and ran back to the hotel. But people forget that when he went to England the first time the people didn't like him. They thought he was too much of a loudmouth."

'Enery's 'Ammer, a wicked left hook to the chin, dumped him on his regal ass in the fourth round and Britain sensed an upset. But for the bell intervening to end the round, who knows what might have been? With his fighter's senses scrambled, the

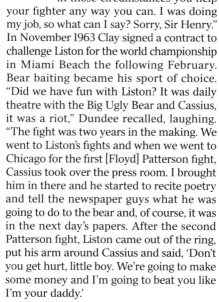

Ali loved to fight and he loved to train. He was a joy

quickest thinker was Dundee. "It's a myth that I gained my guy an extra five or six minutes by causing such a commotion in the corner and making the secretary of the British Boxing Board of Control send to the dressing rooms for a new pair of gloves. But he got a few extra seconds before the bell rang for the fifth round and this was all the time in the world in the circumstances. When he staggered back to the corner — with my guidance because I jumped in the ring as soon as the bell rang — he looked out of it. Chickie Ferrara got to work with the smelling salts under his nose and ice down his pants and I suddenly thought of the small split along the seam of one of his gloves that I had noticed when putting the gloves on him in the dressing room. So I stuck my little pinkie into the tear and made it bigger and that's when I called over the referee [Tommy Little] and any official-looking guy I could lay my eyes on around the ring to come over and examine this defective glove. 'We need a new pair of gloves,' I yelled.

"Cassius is coming round, the officials are in a state of flux and, finally, the referee says to me that there are no other gloves. 'Don't worry,' I told him. 'These will be fine.' My guy didn't need minutes to recover, as I have seen reported, but those few seconds of pandemonium added to the minute's rest were vital. He came out for the fifth round fully recovered and, within seconds of the resumption, he worsened the cuts around Cooper's eyes and before you knew it, the fight was over. The referee stopped it because of the blood which was pouring down Cooper's face. Hey, in those circumstances you help your fighter any way you can. I was doing my job, so what can I say? Sorry, Sir Henry."

In November 1963 Clay signed a contract to challenge Liston for the world championship in Miami Beach the following February. Bear baiting became his sport of choice. "Did we have fun with Liston? It was daily theatre with the Big Ugly Bear and Cassius, it was a riot," Dundee recalled, laughing. "The fight was two years in the making. We went to Liston's fights and when we went to Chicago for the first [Floyd] Patterson fight, Cassius took over the press room. I brought him in there and he started to recite poetry and tell the newspaper guys what he was going to do to the bear and, of course, it was in the next day's papers. After the second Patterson fight, Liston came out of the ring, put his arm around Cassius and said, 'Don't you get hurt, little boy. We're going to make some money and I'm going to beat you like I'm your daddy.'

"Muhammad loved the winding-up of an opponent as much as he loved the fight." Nothing wound up Liston more than the night Clay arrived at his home in Denver at 2am. "He started shouting, 'Come out, you big ugly bear. Come out and face me.' Woke up the whole neighbourhood and Sonny wasn't pleased. He was wearing pyjamas and a night gown when he came storming out of his front door wielding a poker. I dread to think what he'd have done if he had laid his hands on him but Muhammad was too fast and he quickly got back in the bus."

The 22-year-old challenger destroyed the aura of invincibility that surrounded his opponent. "Liston used to play it up like he was a big man, a monster," Dundee said. "He had a little guy working with him who was shorter than me and he used to put towels under his robe to make him look even bigger. I told my guy when he walked across the ring to make sure to stand tall, put both feet together and look him in the eye. He

Below

Dundee's relationship with Ali spanned more than half a century

did, he looked right into Liston's eyes and he told him, 'Now I got you, sucker.' He got to Liston in the first round, busted him up under the eye with a hard punch, and it was like Sonny grew old overnight.

"The second fight in Maine, when he knocked out Liston in round one, people called it the phantom punch but that was a projected move — slide over and boom! The guy didn't see the punch. Winning the title in Miami Beach was a special night. We had no party after because I never believed in post-fight parties and the kid didn't drink alcohol. Besides, his whole life was a party. He used to say that he was living his movie every morning he got up and so he was."

Reflecting on Ali's life after boxing, Dundee said: "In his heart he was always a happy

human being. Everybody will remember Muhammad Ali. Forever. I have gone to places, little places, and they knew me because of Muhammad. It's a nice feeling. But it's a heartbreaker when you know a guy from when he was a boy and you see him with Parkinson's.

"I have all those memories. The days up at his camp in Deer Lake, when he drew people to the place like bees to honey. Gene Kilroy, who was responsible for buying the camp, brought him to a nursing home once and an elderly man looked up and smiled at him. 'Joe Louis?' he inquired. All his life he had wanted to meet Joe Louis. Ali shook his hand and signed an autograph: 'Glad I finally had the opportunity to meet you ... Joe Louis.' Wasn't he something?"

GOLDEN YEARS

1964 -1967

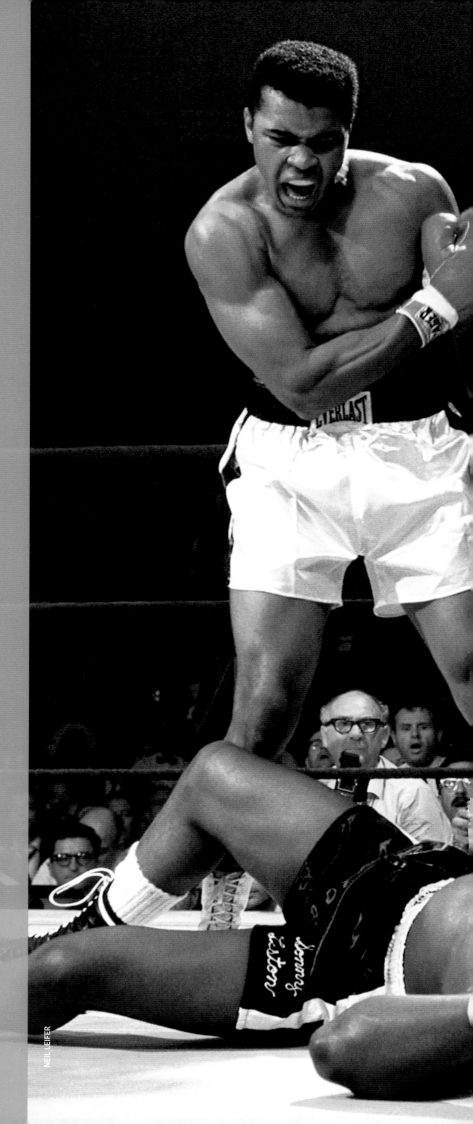

Sonny Liston is nothing. The man can't talk. The man can't fight. The man needs talking lessons. The man needs boxing lessons. And since he's gonna fight me, he needs falling lessons

CASSIUS CLAY TALKS THE TALK BEFORE BEATING WORLD CHAMPION LISTON IN 1964

NEIL LEIFER

THE UGLY SIDE OF BEAUTY

The Greatest was a far more complicated figure than the sanitised version fed to the public in recent years.
By **Matthew Syed**

orman Mailer, perhaps his most eloquent chronicler, once described Muhammad Ali as "beautiful". "There is always a shock in seeing him again," Mailer wrote in his seminal book *The Fight*. "Not live as in television but standing before you, looking his best. Then the World's Greatest Athlete is in danger of being our most beautiful man . . .Women draw an audible breath. Men look down . . . If Ali never opened his mouth to quiver the jellies of public opinion, he would still inspire love and hate. For he is the Prince of Heaven — so says the silence around his body when he is luminous."

Ali was, indeed, beautiful. In the way he moved, the way he talked, and in the high-voltage charisma that seemed to flow whenever he stood near a TV camera, he redefined the nature of 20th-century celebrity. He could box, too. When he took on Cleveland Williams in 1966 at the height of his powers, he altered the way many observers thought about sport. He danced and glided, connecting with 100 punches and taking just three. As one pundit put it: "This is the closest sport has come to perfection. For seven or so

minutes, Ali turned boxing into ballet". But Ali was not always beautiful. He could be ugly, vindictive and, at times, hypocritical. Indeed, the only way to fully understand how a "mere" sportsman rose to become one of the most influential figures of the last century, you have to engage with both the light and the darkness.

Above
Muhammad Ali shows off a journal by Nation of Islam at Howard university

Above left
Malcolm X stands behind Muhammad Ali, a week after the boxer beat Sonny Liston to become world champion

Over recent decades, particularly since his descent caused by Parkinson's syndrome, the image of Ali has been carefully sanitised. He was positioned by his commercial handlers as saintly, unifying, pacifistic and unthreatening. But the real Ali, the man who shocked, outraged, fascinated and ultimately endeared the world, was a polarising and controversial figure. In his words and deeds, there was always a whiff of Semtex. Now, more than ever, it is time to rediscover the real Ali.

His arrival on the world stage can be pinned to a particular date: February 25, 1964. Ali had already won Olympic gold in the light-heavyweight event in Rome, but it was his challenge for the so-called richest prize in sport that transformed him into a cultural icon. Few gave this unorthodox pugilist, who carried his hands low, a hope. Three of 40-plus ringside journalists picked Cassius Clay, as he was called, to defeat Sonny Liston, the defending champion. Of all of Ali's title bouts, this remains the most electric. He edged the contest until the 4th, when an illegal substance from Liston's glove found its way into his eyes. Almost blinded, Ali kept Liston at bay by holding his arms out horizontally, but as his vision began to clear, he started to dominate. Liston seemed to age as Ali danced around him and he failed to answer the bell for the 7th round (some observers claim he was ordered to throw the contest by the mob). It was a breathtaking performance. As Ferdie Pacheco, his long-time doctor put it: "Beethoven wrote some of his greatest symphonies when he was deaf. Why couldn't Cassius Clay fight when he was blind?"

It wasn't until the next day, however, that the story shifted to the front pages. Ali informed a press conference that he had converted to the Nation of Islam, an extremist, anti-white religious group. He also said that he had dropped his "slave name" (Cassius Clay was, in fact, the name of a 19th-century abolitionist). Soon afterwards, he became Muhammad Ali. Mainstream America, accustomed to compliant black athletes in the mould of Joe Louis, the former heavyweight champion, was outraged. The Nation had a surrealist theology, preaching that blacks were the first humans and that whites had been created in a botched experiment conducted by a rogue scientist. They also believed that blacks would be rescued from a looming apocalypse by a wheel-shaped spaceship.

But it was their political vision that caused the deepest anxiety. They argued for a separation between the races, campaigning aggressively (and with a stated belief in the use of force) for a homeland for blacks within the borders of the United States. That put them in direct opposition to the integrationist agenda of Martin Luther King and, curiously enough, on the same page as white supremacist groups, who also believed in racial segregation. Soon after his conversion, Ali himself addressed a meeting of the Ku Klux Klan, saying: "Blue birds with blue birds, red birds with red birds, pigeons with pigeons, eagles with eagles! God didn't make no mistake!"

How could Ali have fraternised with an organisation that had lynched and murdered across the former Confederacy? How could he associate with people whose declared aim was to create a state of terror among blacks south of the Mason-Dixon Line? To his detractors, then and now, Ali was a racist, pure and simple. He believed that whites were congenitally evil, just as the

A speech by Elijah Muhammad at a Nation of Islam convention receives applause from its most famous member

Muhammad Ali kisses the Koran

Klan believed that blacks were congenitally subhuman. In multiple interviews, Ali proclaimed his ideology. "We cannot live in harmony because we are different," he said. "Whites have a bad nature, they cannot be trusted . . . We need to have our own land, our own government, our own way of doing things." Mark Kram, in his book Ghosts of Manila, wrote: "Seldom has a public figure of such superficial depth been more wrongly perceived — by the right and the left. Today, he would be looked upon as a contaminant, a chronic user of hate language."

But the context of Ali's views should not be overlooked. He grew up in Louisville,

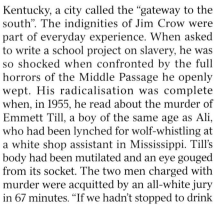

Above
World heavyweight champion Muhammad Ali rides a horse near the pyramids in Giza, Egypt, in 1964

Blue birds with blue birds, red birds with red birds, pigeons with pigeons, eagles with eagles

Kentucky, a city called the "gateway to the south". The indignities of Jim Crow were part of everyday experience. When asked to write a school project on slavery, he was so shocked when confronted by the full horrors of the Middle Passage he openly wept. His radicalisation was complete when, in 1955, he read about the murder of Emmett Till, a boy of the same age as Ali, who had been lynched for wolf-whistling at a white shop assistant in Mississippi. Till's body had been mutilated and an eye gouged from its socket. The two men charged with murder were acquitted by an all-white jury in 67 minutes. "If we hadn't stopped to drink

pop, it wouldn't have taken so long", one juror said.

From this perspective, Ali's demonisation of whites can at least be understood, if not condoned. The Black Muslims may have had a similar ideology to the Klan on paper but the historical context could not have been more different. The Klan wished to sustain a reign of hatred against blacks in the South. The anti-white racism of the Nation of Islam was more a cry for help, the vigilante response of an impotent and pitiful minority. Either way, there is no doubt that Ali's position as heavyweight champion handed the Nation a political

BETTMANN/KEYSTONE

ALI   27

significance out of all proportion to their small base. For a brief period, the fear of a rising black underclass, disciplined, well organised, and intent on insurrection, struck fear into Middle America. And it was at this moment that Luther King played his trump card. Concerned that the Civil Rights Bill was bogged down in Congress, he realised that the extremist rhetoric of the new heavyweight champion might be used to secure concessions. In one of his biggest political gambles, he painted a chilling vision of what might happen if reforms were delayed further, pushing more young blacks into the arms of the extremists.

In a watershed article in the *Chicago Defender*, Jackie Robinson, the first black player to cross the colour line in Major League Baseball, made the case. "I don't think Negroes en masse will embrace Black Muslimism any more than they have communism. Young and old, Negroes by the tens of thousands went into the streets of America and proved their willingness to suffer, to fight, and even die for their freedom. These people want more democracy — not less. They want to be integrated into the mainstream of American life, not invited to live in some small cubicle

of this land in splendid isolation. If Negroes ever turn to the Black Muslim movement, in any numbers, it will not be because of Cassius Clay or even Malcolm X. It will be because white America has refused to recognise the responsible leadership of the Negro people and to grant us the same rights that any other citizen enjoys."

President Johnson got the point, strengthening the act against the wishes of his party. The 1964 Bill went further than anyone had believed possible only months earlier and, along with the Voting Rights Act in 1965, banned employment discrimination and obliterated the disenfranchisement of blacks throughout the South. It is a deep irony of Ali's life that in allying himself with a creed fanatically opposed to integration, he smoothed the passage of the most seminal integrationist legislation in American history. Jim Crow had finally expired.

America was a-changin', and, soon, Ali was changing too. By 1967, he had defended the title nine times (including a rematch with Liston), almost without breaking sweat. And yet, even as the nation was starting to warm to a man they had previously vilified, he took a stance that would divide

Below

John W Milam and Roy Bryant sit with their children as they await trial for the 'wolf whistle' murder of black teenager Emmett Till, above

it again. His refusal to accept the draft for Vietnam was another calculated act of hostility against the establishment. "I ain't got no quarrel with them Viet Cong", Ali said. The words would ultimately become a rallying cry for critics of the war, but at the time it still commanded support and his stance was regarded as an act of betrayal. The boxing authorities stripped him of his title, and he spent three and a half years in the wilderness. By the time he returned, however, the world had shifted. Opinion had swung against the war, and Ali was on the verge of being embraced by mainstream America for the first time. His courage convinced many of his severest critics that he was a man of principle whose stances pierced the surface assumptions of American society. He even won his case against the United States government, avoiding jail and garnering an apology.

In 1974, as he travelled to Zaire to take on George Foreman for the heavyweight title (he had been defeated by Joe Frazier in his first attempt to regain the championship in 1971), he had become a hero to millions at home and abroad. It was a stunning turnaround. He was, by now, the most famous person on the planet, able to

> "We cannot live in harmony because we are different. Whites have a bad nature, they cannot be trusted"

charm and delight audiences with effortless charisma. For the US, still traumatised by Watergate and Vietnam, these mega-bouts offered much-needed escapism. The pre-bout vaudeville and hype became essential to the drumbeat of the Seventies.

To many, the 1974 clash with Foreman remains Ali's definitive bout. However, he was way past his best. Three and a half years out of the ring had created a much slower boxer. Ali called his tactics against Foreman "rope-a-dope", taking mighty shots on his body and arms that would have previously hit thin air. He won with a stoppage in the 8th round, but urinated blood for weeks afterwards. After the savage, 14-round epic with Frazier in the Philippines, the fabled Thrilla in Manila in 1975, he looked as if he had been in a traffic accident. But America loved him for it. He took punishment. He bled. For some people, this represented heroism.

Within months of his retirement in 1981, the signs of Parkinson's were already manifest. The descent into illness had begun. For most of the rest of his life, Ali lived a curious half-life, both in the spotlight and beyond it. He renounced the Nation and converted to moderate form of Sunni Islam. Gradually, however, the melodious voice was silenced. An 80 per cent share in his name, image and likeness were sold for $50m to CKX, an entertainment conglomerate, which started the process of airbrushing his image.

He was positioned, doubtless for commercial reasons, as a Gandhi-like caricature who preached peace and tolerance. The real Ali, the man whose explosive stances subtly altered American history, was drowned in a deluge of misleading sentimentality. In the eyes of a new generation, Ali was a teddy bear: safe, unthreatening and devoid of the contradictions that symbolised post-war American consciousness.

Yet only a historian lacking imagination could fail to place Ali among the most influential figures of the last century. He was a sportsman with a conscience, a man whose desire to right the injustices in society led him down many roads, both dark and light.

In his life, we glimpse not only the moral complexity of the most transformative epoch in modern American history, but also the story of a boy from a small town who, against all odds,"shook up the world". He was imperfect and flawed, courageous and so very beautiful.

He was, unquestionably, The Greatest.

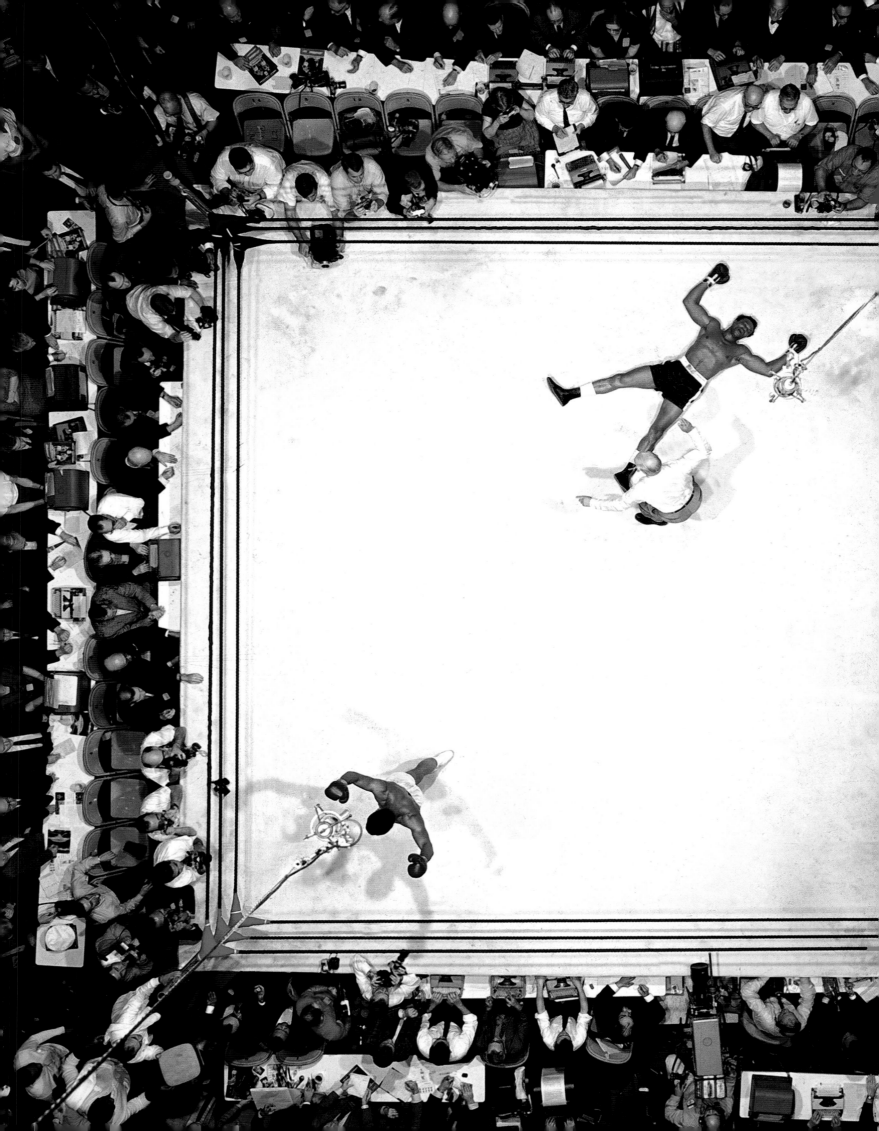

NEIL LEIFER

CAUTION: GENIUS AT WORK

In just three rounds, Ali produced one of his most brilliant performances

Houston was the venue for a virtuoso display from Muhammad Ali in 1966. His opponent Cleveland Williams, known as the Big Cat, was tamed by Ali in what the sports writer Hugh McIlvanney has called "the greatest exhibition of boxing virtuosity he ever produced". Contemporary reports of the fight reflected Ali's brilliance: A bout with Ernie Terrell (recognised as champion by the World Boxing Association) was the next on the horizon for Muhammad Ali, the world heavyweight champion, after he had beaten Cleveland Williams in 7min 8sec last night, *The Times reported on November 16*. In his most impressive performance, the 24-year-old showed dazzling speed, punching power and a quality lacking in his previous bouts — the "killer instinct".

Williams, 33, was down three times in the second round and once in the third before the referee, Harry Kessler, stopped the contest. When Terrell visited Ali's dressing room, Ali shouted: "You're next."

The knock-downs were achieved by perfectly timed left-and-right combinations to the head. The third, in the second round, stretched Williams flat on his back. Only the bell saved him. Dragged to his stool by his handlers, Williams went out on wobbly legs for the third round and was soon down again. He staggered up, but Kessler stopped the bout.

Kessler said Ali punched with more power than he had shown in his previous contests. "He moved well. I had to stop the fight. Williams' knees were rubbery and his eyes were glassy."

Ali said: "He never landed a punch on me, just a couple of light jabs. Williams seemed to be a target, because I was extra fast."

Williams reflected: "He hit me before I had a chance to hit him. I dropped my left hand and he nailed me."

Left

Cleveland Williams lies flat on his back after a fearsome onslaught in 1966

"

Williams went out on wobbly legs and was knocked down again

OUT OF ACTION

1967-1970

Man, I ain't got no quarrel with them Viet Cong. No Viet Cong ever called me nigger

SPEAKING AFTER FINDING OUT HE WAS TO BE DRAFTED BY THE US ARMY

'MY TEN DAYS BEHIND BARS'

While the threat of prison hung over **Muhammad Ali** when he refused to fight in Vietnam, he was jailed in 1968 for a traffic violation

Even in exile I'm surrounded by people. I've never spent a night in jail. Could I accept the confinement? It is this thinking that causes me to make a move to test myself, even in a small way. The chance comes when a motorcycle policeman follows me down a Miami street and pulls me over to the side.

"Are you Muhammad Ali?"

"Yes, sir. I am, sir."

"There's a warrant out for your arrest." He explains that they've been looking for me for an old traffic violation for a year. "Follow me," he says.

And I follow him into what will eventually turn out to be a ten-day sentence in the Miami Dade County Jail.

I walk in to surrender myself. They're surprised to see me. I'm fingerprinted and given some prison clothes, and before I'm assigned to my cell a short red-faced official says, "Since you gave yourself up on your own, we won't treat you like a common criminal. We'll let you choose your own work detail. Either laundry, the yard, the shop or the cafeteria."

I choose the cafeteria because an old convict in Chicago once told me it's the best place for a new prisoner, and I follow the guard to my cell. It's the size of four ordinary bedrooms, except there's no furniture – just steel bunks covered with plastic mattresses and flimsy sheets and old army blankets. In the corner a face bowl and toilet. When I walk in, the door slams behind me and locks. I put my hands on the bars, look down the hall. The strangest feeling comes over me. I remind myself it's only for a few days.

"It's Muhammad Ali, The Champ! Hey!" Inmates in my own cell and the ones across the way begin jumping off their bunks, shouting, "Champ, what you doing here? Muhammad Ali, welcome home!"

When the lights go out, I lie on my bed, but I can't sleep. I think half the night about the people on the outside, about places I've been but what I miss most is my wife and daughter Maryum. I think of what would happen to them if my appeal is lost and I'm forced to live this way for five years. The thought gnaws on me until I drift off.

The next day, I go to the kitchen and do what I'm told. One of the cooks, a tall, thin black prisoner in his mid-thirties, comes up and welcomes me in Arabic. When I recognise his greeting, he apologises and says, "I'm not a Muslim, but I studied a lot about it. A lot of prisoners joined since they been here. Can you take this for five years, brother?"

"If I have to," I tell him.

GETTY IMAGES

Below left
The media gather around Muhammad Ali as he goes to court to face trial in Houston in 1967 because of his refusal to be drafted

Below
A letter written by Ali to the selective service board stating that he was a conscientious objector to the Vietnam War

> When the lights go out what I miss most is my wife and daughter

He shakes his head. "But you don't have to. That's the hard part, you don't have to. Just by changing your mind you can be out from under." He winks.

After dinner we sit in our cells and talk. There's a debate going on over the radio about whether Dade Jail should allow all prisoners Christmas amnesty. "Everyone should get out for Christmas except that draft-dodger," one woman is telling the moderator. "The only way they should let him out is send him to Vietnam." "Muslims don't celebrate Christmas," a man calls in. "Keep him there!" It's known all over Miami that I'm one of the prisoners.

In the morning the guard is banging on the bars: "The judge has declared a Christmas amnesty! A Christmas amnesty!" A yell and a roar goes up through the cell blocks. Some begin chanting Christmas carols.

"Does it cover me?" I ask.

He looks down the sheet and finally grins. "You on it too, Champ. The judge had a hard time getting you off. Threats on his life, threats against his family because they wanted you to stay in jail."

He opens up my cell, takes me to a room where the little red-faced man pulls out a cashbox and hands me two dollar bills. "You're free now," the man says. I'm halfway down the hall and out of the building when a prisoner rushes up: "You dropped your money." I tell him to keep it.

I never knew the smell of fresh air was so good. I start walking and somehow I don't want to stop. I look at the faces of people on the streets and I can't get enough of seeing them. I look at the cars passing by, the grass, the trees, the birds. I see children and I hear their voices come up to me: "Hey! Champ!", "That's Muhammad Ali." They run over, ask for autographs, and I sign. When I get to the hotel, I strip down and lay on the bed. I prop my head up on a pillow for the first time in a week. I want to sleep.

Extracted from The Greatest: My Own Story by Muhammad Ali with Richard Durham (Graymalkin Media)

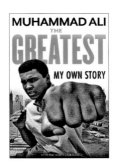

Local Board reopening my classification so that my claim for ex-emption as a minister of religion, which has never before been submitted to the Local Board, may be determined and if necessary the Appeal Boards be given an opportunity to decide whether I am entitled to exemption as a minister of religion as requested in my letter to reopen classification dated August 23, 1966, and addressed to Local Board No. 47, Louisville, Kentucky.

Respectfully submitted,

CASSIUS MARCELLUS CLAY, JR.
a/k/a MUHAMMAD ALI
Special Field Minister
The Lost Found Nation of Islam

HE WAS RIGHT TO SAY NO

Refusing to fight for his country was a matter of principle, according to **Lonnie Ali**, the boxer's fourth wife

Throughout Muhammad's entire career, there were people saying to him, "Muhammad, just make this one compromise with principle. Muhammad, just make that one change in your beliefs". And each one, if he'd made it, would have taken away from who he was. But he always held firm; he's a better person for it. And I think this country is a better country because of his struggle, particularly as it related to Vietnam.

That war wasn't about serving the United States. It wasn't about national defence. This country wasn't under attack. It had to do with America prowling around in other people's affairs. And Muhammad was right. Back in the 1960s, black people didn't have justice in America. We didn't have a full place here. We were still slaves — mentally, if not legally. There were places in this country where Muhammad couldn't even sit at a lunch counter, and yet he was expected to go to Asia and annihilate people who'd never done anything wrong to him. The Viet Cong had never done anything to Muhammad. There were white people here in America who did a lot to him every day and he wasn't at war with white people in America, so why should he go to war with people overseas?

That was his frame of mind, and I think it was true of most other black Americans at that time, but Muhammad stood up for his beliefs. He didn't flee to Canada. He didn't take any other circuitous route, honourable or dishonourable. He just said, "I'm not going, and if you want to lock me up, go ahead and do it". That took a lot of courage. He wasn't subjected to gunfire, but in his own way, it took as much courage as the people who went out there to fight. He was threatened with jail; his livelihood was taken away; people called him a traitor and worse. You have no way of knowing the ridicule Muhammad faced and how badly hurt he was by some of the things people said about him. But he never stopped believing in this country or the essential good of its people. He would have been mentally destroyed if he'd gone to Vietnam.

Given the type of person he is — his compassion, his decency — Muhammad wouldn't have come back from that experience whole. Muhammad could never pick up a rifle and kill someone. This man was never capable of shooting another person. He won't even hunt. He can't kill an animal, so how could you expect him to kill another human being? All it would have taken was for Muhammad to see one person shot and killed, one child dead, I don't care what side they were on, and it would have destroyed him."

Edited extract from Muhammad Ali: His Life and Times by Thomas Hauser, published by Portico

He would have been mentally destroyed if he'd gone to Vietnam

THE RETURN

1970-1975

I've seen
George Foreman
shadow-boxing
and the
shadow won

ALI IN CONFIDENT MOOD BEFORE FIGHTING
FOREMAN IN 1974. HE WON IN EIGHT ROUNDS

CHRIS SMITH

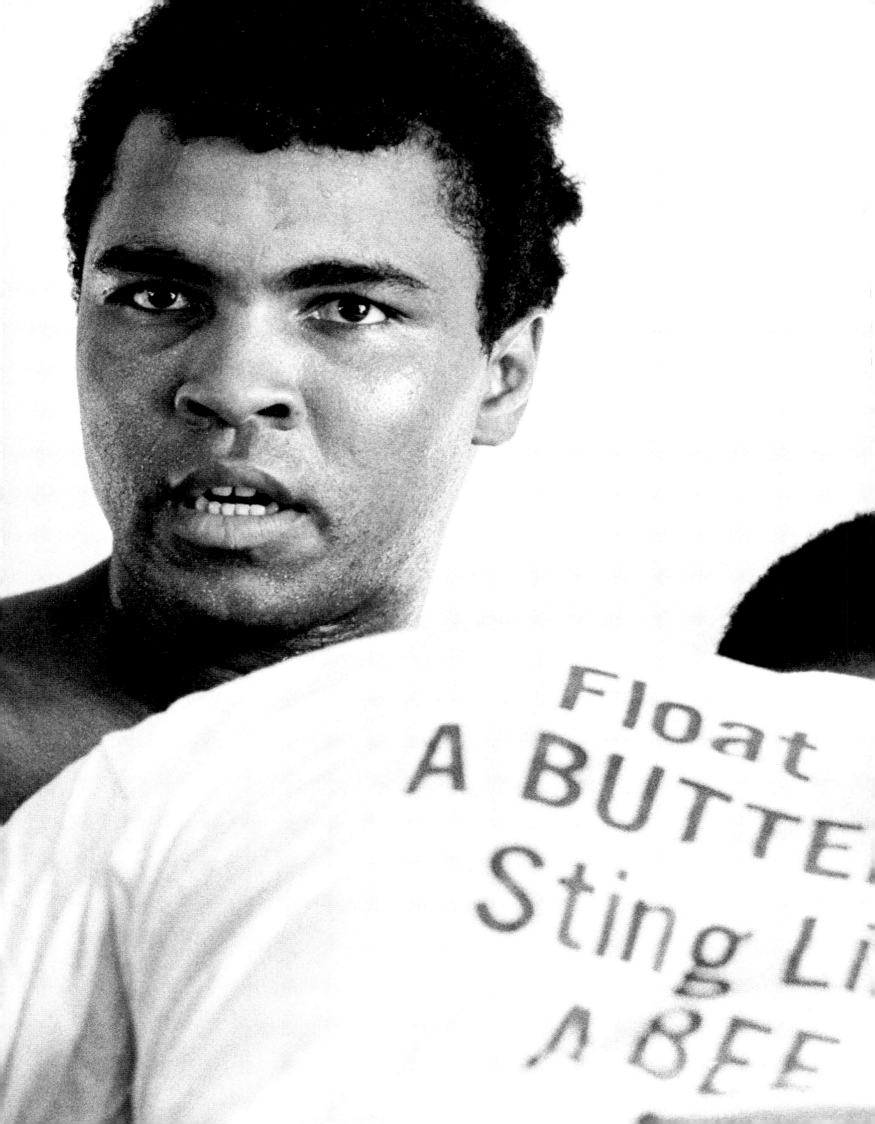

TRAINING
ALI STYLE

A typical day saw the champion burn 2,375 calories during his workout

1 Running
Ali would get up at 5.30am and run six miles to training wearing heavy army boots in under 40 minutes
Calories burned: 650

2 Warm-up stretches
15 minutes including side-to-sides, torso swivels, jumping around on toes to limber up
Calories burned: 125

3 Shadow-boxing
5 x 3 minute rounds, working on footwork and speed punching (30-second break in between rounds)
Calories burned: 320

4 Heavy bag
6 X 3 minute rounds, working on stamina and combinations (30-second break in between rounds)

Calories burned: 505

5 Floor exercises
15 minutes (around 300 exercises in total). Bicycle crunches, sit-ups with medicine ball, leg raises

Calories burned: 230

6 Speed Bag
9 minutes (1 minute break)

Calories burned: 145

7 Skipping
20 minutes (Ali always moved around while skipping, never staying in the same spot)

Calories burned: 360

8 Shadow-boxing
1 minute, walking around with light shadow boxing as a cooling-down session

Calories burned: 40

GETTING DOWN TO BUSINESS

Darren Smith reveals what it took for Ali to become The Greatest

Want to fight like the great Muhammad Ali? First you have to train like him. When Muhammad Ali met Neil Allen in a little west London gym in 1966, he chatted with The Times' boxing and athletics correspondent about the importance of road work in preparation for his fights. 'Everyone's talking about mah style, mah speed and all that's natural to me. Well I may have been given both mental and physical gifts, but you still got to work yourself hard.'

And work hard he did. Angelo Dundee was an old school trainer, and for six days a week he would work Ali to the point of exhaustion. A reporter once asked Ali how many sit-ups he did, to which Ali replied "I don't know. I only start counting when they start to hurt." Despite the pain, Dundee never had to ask Ali to come to the gym – he was there before the gym opened. He was the first to arrive and the last to leave. He did the longest and hardest workouts.

Surprisingly, Ali never used weights in training: he and Dundee believed that 'excess' muscle would slow his punches, so they avoided the 'bulking' exercises and focused on the classics to improve core strength, speed and fluidity: running, crunches, push-ups, squats, speed bag training, and skipping.

For Ali speed and endurance was everything. He firmly believed that the fight is not won in the ring, but away from the spotlight, away from the crowds, in the gym, when no one is watching. His

Ali believed that the fight is not won in the ring, but away from the spotlight

endurance training paid off: in round seven of the 'Rumble in the Jungle' against George Foreman in 1974, Ali clinched George and yelled: "You got eight more rounds to go, sucker . . . I ain't even started. Look at you! Out of gas and I'm whippin' you." Foreman was exhausted: his punches were weaker, his breathing laboured. By round eight the fight was over.

We have prepared a typical training regime that Ali performed six days a week above. See if you can follow it. You can't just proclaim that you're "The Greatest'". Greatness has to be earned.

Left
Muhammad Ali trains on the heavy bag before a fight against Brian London in 1966

Right
Classic exercises such as sit-ups form the core of the boxer's vigorous training regime

HANDS

PIERRE HOULES

This is a life-size picture of Muhammad Ali and George Foreman's fists taken before their fight in 1974. To grasp their sheer size, hold yours up against theirs

WIDTH OF ALI'S FIST (THE ONE ON THE RIGHT) IS 14.5 CM

ALI
— v —
FRAZIER

FIGHT 1

MADISON SQUARE GARDEN, NEW YORK
MARCH 8, 1971

When his swollen face has healed, Ali, perhaps no longer the greatest but a remarkable man in defeat, will seek a return bout for the world heavyweight championship against Joe Frazier, who beat him over 15 rounds of brutal, occasionally bizarre but always absorbing boxing, *Neil Allen wrote for The Times.*

Subject to any somewhat unlikely retirement from Frazier there could be a return in Inglewood, California, where Jack Kent Cooke has the promotional option. Not just because of the sums of money which could again be involved, but because Ali has so far proved to be able to make adversity almost as welcome as success. His body has been hurt more than he ever imagined but the spirit of the man seems to flicker brightly enough. Frazier behaved with great dignity when he was interviewed. As he walked past me, he said: "I tell you I feel stronger than when I went in." Then he added: "But he's a good man. He's hard to hurt. I was amazed what he took. I went right back home to get those shots that I finally got to him with."

Of course Ali lost partially because he has had to be three years away from the ring. But there are riders to that excuse. I am convinced that never before did he meet anyone as good as Frazier. Ali remains the stylist whom every schoolboy boxer, who wishes to end up still looking his mother's son, should follow. But in professional boxing perhaps his problem, apart from the draft issue, has been that he was such a great natural athlete he sometimes neglected a few basic truths about the sport. But who can tell what he may yet to teach us now that he intends to go on?

Frazier won by unanimous decision

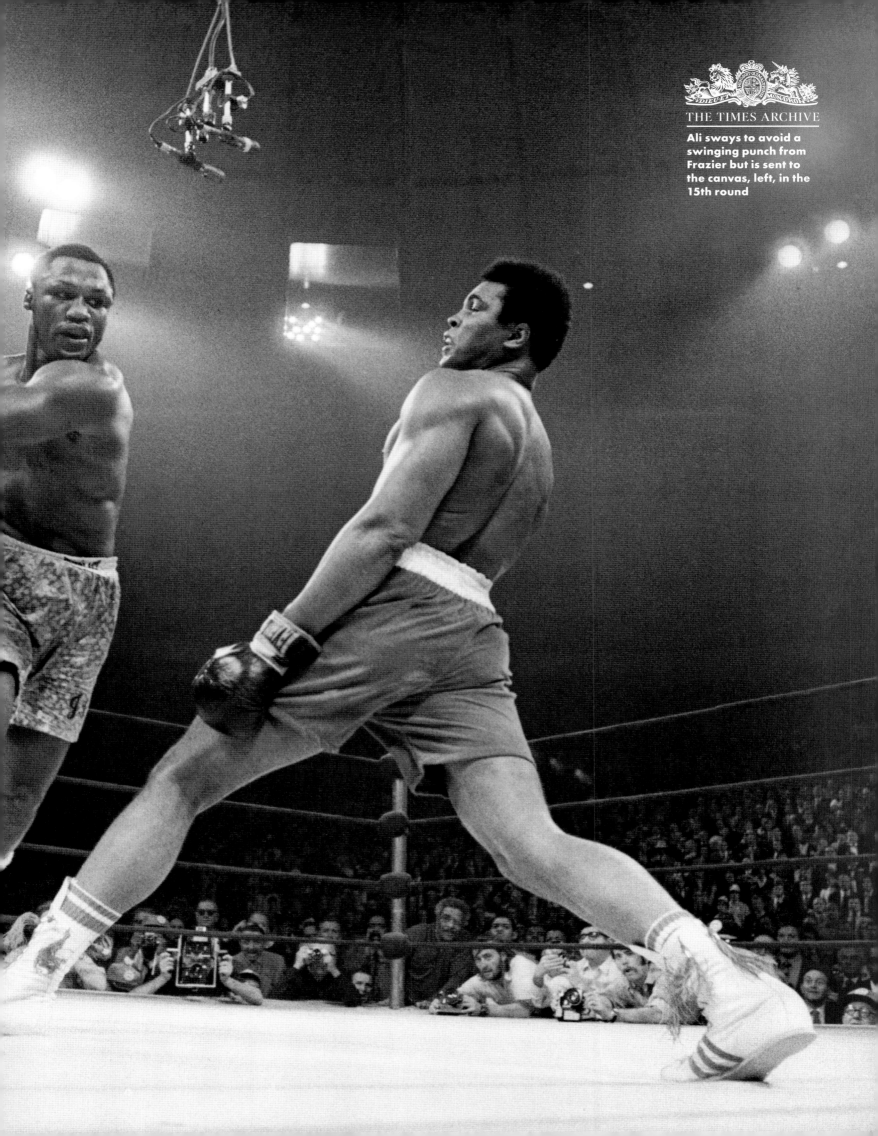

ALI
— v —
FRAZIER

FIGHT 2

MADISON SQUARE GARDEN, NEW YORK
JANUARY 28, 1974

For all the thousands around them, the former world champions looked intensely lonely as they climbed into the ring, *Rex Bellamy reported for The Times*. Ali straight yet supple, Frazier a quivering assembly of excited muscles. Ali was the first into his stride. He showed us his famous shuffle. He stayed in one place long enough to land a flurry of punches, then danced out of range. He needed to. Frazier's left was threatening to make dents in Ali's superb physique.

Two judges gave the third round to Frazier, he was landing more often. Ali was beginning to hit and hold rather than hit and run. Ali won the sixth. True, he showed off a little (the shuffle, the briefly proffered open target). But I felt that, as with Ilie Nastase on a tennis court, a little teasing fun was an essential component of his best form.

The seventh and eighth rounds were Frazier's best. Ali could not hit him often enough to evade him quickly enough. The weight of Frazier's punches was appallingly hurtful. "He's really whacking him," muttered a man from Barnsley, bringing some homespun English into an alien context.

The 10th was probably Frazier's, the 11th certainly Ali's. At the end, they were locked in each other's arms once again. After the bell, Frazier paced about like a caged animal. He still had a lot of punches to throw, but had nowhere to throw them. At the end of his press conference, a strange blend of conversational comments and hectoring speeches, Ali declaimed a poem entitled Truth. We wondered if the poet understood his own message. Ali has not provided proof that he is a better man than Frazier: a fighter George Foreman put away in two rounds.

Ali won by unanimous decision

THE TIMES ARCHIVE

Frazier comes under
attack in round 12.
Ali prepared for
the showdown in
Pennsylvania, left

ALI
— v —
FOREMAN

THE RUMBLE IN THE JUNGLE

STADE DU 20 MAI, KINSHASA, ZAIRE
OCTOBER 31, 1974

S o the good news for boxing is that the once and future king will be with us for a while as all the world marvels at his resilience and courage, *Neil Allen reported for The Times*, As dawn came up over the stadium today, we knew that if we had not seen a great match — it was really too one-sided for that — we had witnessed a classic kill which even the lions up country might envy.

The final left and right punches, as Ali came springing out of a corner, sent Foreman spinning round and down, flat on his back, where he lay, head jerking up like a dying animal, and then sprawling on hands and knees as the referee spread his arms wide.

Ali leaped in triumph and then fell, pushed by a mob invading the ring before he sat on his haunches while pandemonium raged. Helmeted troops beat back the crowd and finally Ali was able to raise his hands to the night sky and urge 60,000 onlookers to cry

"Ali, boom a yea", literally "Ali, kill him". Foreman, his right eye swollen and blood trickling from his nose and mouth, sat hunched in his corner, a bemused, broken man.

It was the matador toying with the bull in the seventh round as Ali burnt in left hands and then dropped home the right. There was one sequence of four successive jabs by Ali with the crowd roaring as each spear sunk home, and Ali looked incredulous at the ease of his task.

Early in the eighth Ali was jolted by three rights to the head as Foreman nervously licked his lips. But Ali came out of a corner with sudden momentum and the next moment the crown had changed hands. Foreman had proved his inexperience in the most painful manner. Ali had proved us wrong in the most exciting way.

Ali won by knockout in round eight

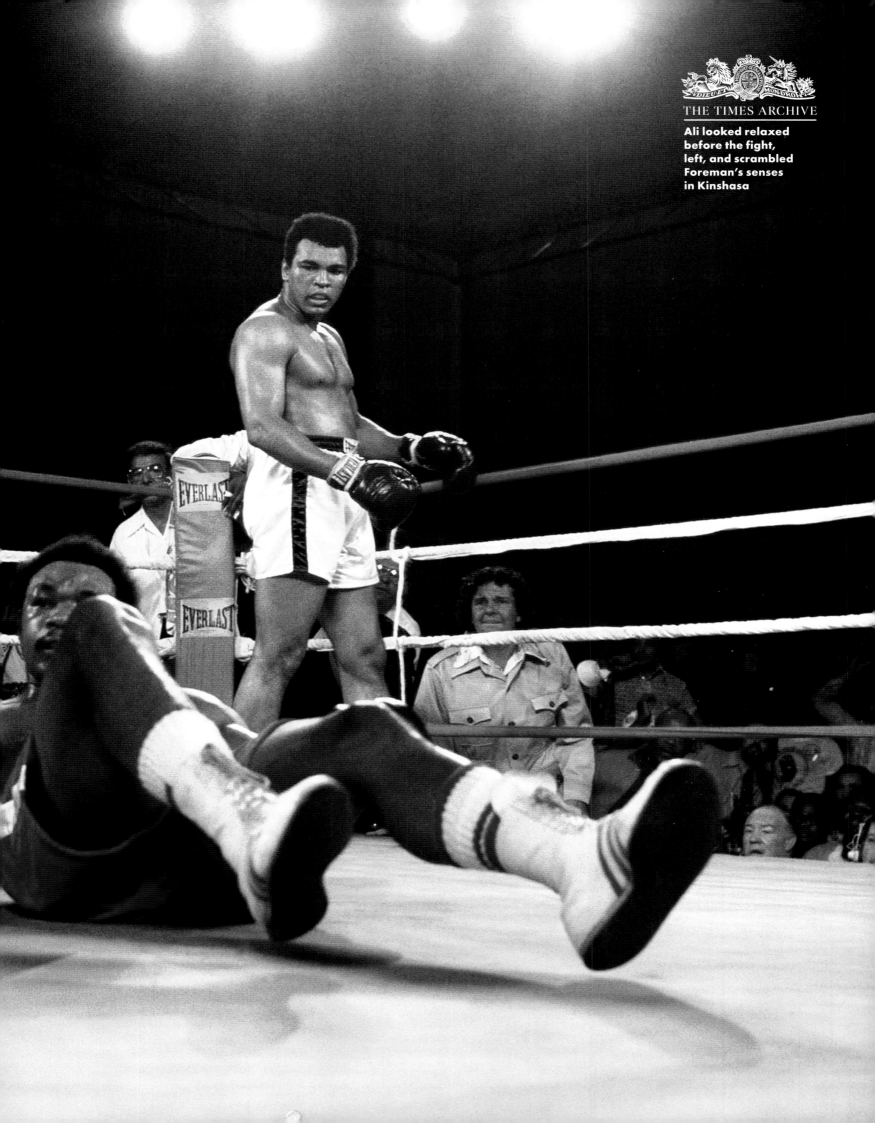

Ali looked relaxed
before the fight,
left, and scrambled
Foreman's senses
in Kinshasa

Ali reflects in training, left. Frazier felt the force of a right-hander in the ninth round

ALI
— v —
FRAZIER

FIGHT 3 - THE THRILLA IN MANILA

ARANETA COLISEUM, QUEZON CITY, PHILIPPINES
OCTOBER 1, 1975

The 41 rounds of brutal conflict which Muhammad Ali and Joe Frazier have endured in their three matches ended with the hardest, most unrelenting heavyweight bout I have ever seen, *Neil Allen reported for The Times.* Watching "the Thrilla from Manila" by live closed circuit television at 4am in London, I found myself on the edge of my seat, gasping at the incredible pace and punishment which Ali and Frazier survived until, thankfully, Frazier was not allowed to come out for the 15th and last round.

Those who were unable to appreciate the psychological lulls of the first Ali-Frazier bout may now well raise their hands in alarm at what the two men did to each other in Quezon City. Of course boxing is an acquired taste which fits uneasily into the 20th century and yesterday's dawn chorus had nothing to offer ornithologists. But for blind courage, for savagely executed punching, for the will to win, I have seen nothing to equal it. Mathematics may seem to have little to do with such a desperate heart against heart encounter. But for what it is worth, when having to rely solely on the screen's view of the action, I gave Ali six rounds, Frazier three and made five rounds even. My BBC radio colleague, Desmond Lynam, sitting next to me with his hands also shaking as he scored, made a similar assessment.

But how impossible it is to calculate the number of blistering two-handed ripostes by Ali, the fearsome left hooks to the liver and jaw by Frazier, the absolute refusal by either to go down, let alone concede defeat. Thank goodness the great egotist had the grace and honesty to say of the battered Frazier: "He is great, he is one hell of a fighter, it was one hell of a fight."

Ali won in round 14 after Frazier's trainer stopped the fight

Whenever people ask me what he was like, I always ask them which Ali they want to talk about — the humorist, the radical activist, the man who fantasised that he could fight every man in the world and beat the lot of them, or the childlike being who loved telling ghost stories.

He was a kaleidoscope of a man quite unlike any other. He lost his temper with me when I challenged him on his sometimes extreme opinions on relations between black and white by pointing out that the writer and commentator Budd Schulberg had written that Ali had more white friends than any other black athlete of Schulberg's acquaintance.

This provoked an outburst of anger and denial which was not feigned and to be honest was frightening, particularly coming as it did from the heavyweight champion of the world.

Strong men wavered in his presence. The actor Liam Neeson, who had boxed a bit and who is not a man you would call a "luvvie", told me that when he met Ali, he shook his hand and found himself saying: "I think I love you."

When I heard he had died I found myself recalling the last time we met in 1980, two months after he had fought Larry Holmes and had been badly beaten.

There were worrying reports about his health. His doctor, Ferdie Pacheco, had resigned, having lost the argument with Ali's advisers that he should stop fighting to avoid serious neurological damage.

A couple of months after losing to Holmes, Ali sat down opposite me in the BBC studios for what was to prove the final, and my favourite, encounter. First impressions were not good. He did not exactly shuffle on to the set but he was slower and bulkier. The physique had thickened and the voice was jaded and slightly slurred.

"I'm tired, man," he said as he sat down, as if to explain what might follow. What did ensue was mellow in comparison to our other encounters. We were both older and more reflective.

I asked him how concerned he was about Pacheco's view that he could end up with brain damage. Pacheco had told him: "You are going to be a shambling wreck."

Ali said: "If I had a low IQ, I'd enjoy this interview."

He went on to argue that the very nature of his profession meant he was a risk-taker. "Look at my face. Twenty-seven years of fighting and not a mark," he said, ignoring the fact that what we could not see and were concerned about was the damage behind the mask.

Ali went on to fight once more. He lost to Trevor Berbick and was punished by a fighter whose presence in the same ring as Ali was in itself the most pertinent indication of the great boxer's decline. Ali

SPARRING ON SCREEN MADE CLASSIC TV

Michael Parkinson, whose interviews with Ali are fondly remembered, believes that the boxer had an indomitable courage, unyielding resolve and a charisma like no other

Above
Muhammad Ali and Michael Parkinson in 1974

Left
Ali raises his guard against Joe Frazier in their 1975 bout, known as the Thrilla in Manila

Arguably the athlete who was boxing's greatest figure is also the sport's biggest tragedy

came under the care of Dr Stanley Fahn, at the Columbia Presbyterian medical centre, who diagnosed Ali's condition as "post-traumatic Parkinsonism due to injuries from fighting".

He is not the first fighter nor will he be the last to have his life blighted by his occupation. We can forever debate who takes the blame but ultimately, in the case of Ali, the real reason he fought for so long was that which made him a great champion — his indomitable courage, unyielding resolve and unquenchable willpower. To expect him to take a careful approach to his life, to work cautiously toward a pension, is to misunderstand the soul of a prizefighter. You might as well require a racehorse to finish its days pulling an ice cream cart.

There are those who need to examine the part they played in observing his downfall and wonder if they could have persuaded him to quit sooner than he did. But then again, Ali told Fahn that he thought the damage had started in the third fight with Frazier in Manila some time before the first manifestation of slurred speech and physical slowing down.

Arguably the athlete who was boxing's greatest figure is also the sport's biggest tragedy. The lesson is that if a fighter as great as Ali can be so badly affected, then no one is safe.

I was asked to present him with his award for the BBC's sportsman of the millennium in 2000 but refused because I felt unable to encounter at close quarters that once glorious man who was now wrecked by a terrible illness.

The fact is that as the years of our acquaintance went by, I grew to admire him more and more and never more than on the last occasion we met when I observed him dealing with his diminishing facilities with great courage and humour. I wanted to remember him as he once was.

"In the history of the world and from the beginning of time, there has never been another fighter like me," Ali once said. Nor, I'll wager, will there ever be.

THAT'S ENTERTAINMENT

ALI AT THE MOVIES
The Greatest (1977): Ali plays himself in an amiable breeze through his life story. Ernest Borgnine stars as Angelo Dundee
Freedom Road (1979): The pugilist tried his hand at acting in this American TV movie about a former slave who becomes a senator. Kris Kristofferson also stars
When We Were Kings (1996): Vivid, atmospheric documentary about 1974's Rumble in the Jungle in Kinshasa
Ali (2002): Will Smith turns on the charisma to play the fighter in drama that looks at his life in and out of the ring. Co-starring Jamie Foxx, Mario Van Peebles and Jon Voight
Soul Power (2009): Footage from the Zaire 74 music festival that helped promote the Kinshasa fight. With Ali, James Brown and Don King involved, there's no lack of ego
Muhammad Ali's Greatest Fight (2013): Dramatisation of the wrangling within the Supreme Court over Ali's refusal to fight in Vietnam. Directed by Brit Stephen Frears

ON RECORD
Cassius Clay released an album, I am the Greatest!, in 1963. It features smatterings of poetry and one catchy song title: Will the Real Sonny Liston Please Fall Down
Songs about the fighter include In Zaire (by Johnny Wakelin), Muhammad Ali (Faithless) and The Ballad of Cassius Clay (The Alcoves)
LL Cool J, below, and Gil Scott-Heron have spoken of the fighter's influence on their music

READING LIST
Muhammad Ali: His Life and Times – Thomas Hauser (Portico)
King of the World – David Remnick (Picador)
McIlvanney on Boxing – Hugh McIlvanney (Mainstream)
The Fight – Norman Mailer (Penguin)
And in a science-fiction world of its own: Superman vs Muhammad Ali – Dennis O'Neil and Neal Adams (DC Comics)
Words by Warren Shore

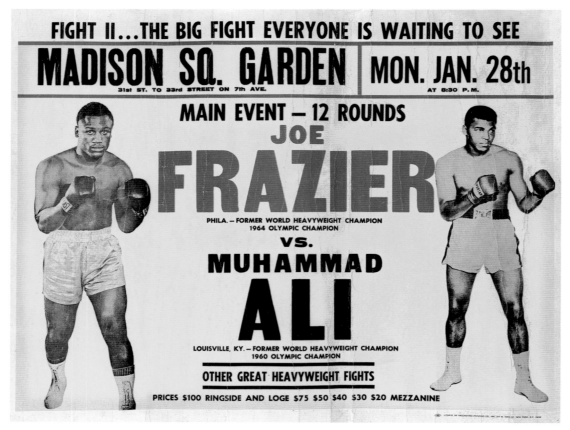

FIGHT II...THE BIG FIGHT EVERYONE IS WAITING TO SEE

MADISON SQ. GARDEN | MON. JAN. 28th
31st ST. TO 33rd STREET ON 7th AVE. | AT 8:30 P.M.

MAIN EVENT — 12 ROUNDS
JOE
FRAZIER
PHILA. — FORMER WORLD HEAVYWEIGHT CHAMPION
1964 OLYMPIC CHAMPION
VS.
MUHAMMAD
ALI
LOUISVILLE, KY. — FORMER WORLD HEAVYWEIGHT CHAMPION
1960 OLYMPIC CHAMPION

OTHER GREAT HEAVYWEIGHT FIGHTS

PRICES $100 RINGSIDE AND LOGE $75 $50 $40 $30 $20 MEZZANINE

Left
Vintage fight posters are in demand, with prices likely to increase since his death

BOXING HISTORY COMES AT A PRICE

It was often said that everybody wanted a piece of Ali and that remains the case when it comes to memorabilia. Almost anything associated with the fighter appeals to fans and collectors, with some items reaching eye-catching amounts at auction.

Gloves worn by Ali for his 1965 fight against Sonny Liston: £650,000

Gloves worn during 1964 fight with Liston: £502,000

Gloves from 1971 clash with Joe Frazier: £237,040

Signed robe worn during training for his final fight, against Trevor Berbick in 1981: £20,400

CASHING IN ON THE CHAMP

The Ali brand can still pack a powerful punch commercially, reports **Iain Dey**

Estimates of Muhammad Ali's wealth are modest in comparison with his worldwide following, but his fortunes had been revived in recent years by a new commercial management deal.

In his prime Ali never attained a level of financial security that matched his boxing prowess and at times his finances were mishandled. A fresh strategy to exploit the boxer's money-making potential was launched three years ago after the Ali family struck a deal with the licensing company Authentic Brands Group (ABG). Three months later, in February 2014, "the Champ" was launched on Twitter to mark the 50th anniversary of his first world title fight against Sonny Liston. ABG, owned in

Right
A businesslike Ali poses with wads of cash at Bank of America in Los Angeles in 1963

part by the British investment company Lion Capital, has commercial rights over Marilyn Monroe and Elvis Presley. It also manages images associated with Michael Jackson and handles the former basketball star Shaquille O'Neal. The deals it has struck for Ali's brand include agreements with the car maker Toyota, the sportswear firm Under Armour and the technology giant Google.

Estimates of his wealth when he died in a Kentucky hospital on June 3 this year ranged from $50m (£35m) to $80m. Reports since his death indicate that there are disagreements within the Ali family about his financial legacy.

Ali's first management deal when he started out as a professional boxer was a six-year contract with 11 white millionaires — the Louisville Sponsoring Group — based in his home state of Kentucky. Under the guidance of trainer Angelo Dundee, Ali rose up the rankings. "They got the complexions and connections to give me good directions," he once said when asked about his backers. The first fight between Ali and Liston for the world heavyweight championship, in Miami on February 25, 1964, was widely reported to be a financial disaster because of poor ticket sales. Some people claimed this was down to Ali's association with Malcolm X, a divisive figure for middle America who was accused of peddling racial hatred. More conventional retired boxers such as Joe Louis claimed it was Ali's loudmouthed antics that put off fight-goers.

"The most logical explanation for the

problems in Miami Beach was promoter error," wrote Michael Ezra in his book Muhammad Ali: The Making of an Icon. The 720 ringside seats in the so-called Golden Circle sold out, despite the staggering $250 price tag — more than twice the going rate for big fight tickets at the time.

Yet most of the cheap seats were empty as the promoters had pushed those prices even higher, proportionally. "Why would anyone pay $100, a price that would normally put them within spitting distance of the fighters, for a seat 50 yards away from the action?," wrote Ezra.

One of the low financial points in Ali's career came when Joe Frazier is said to have helped him out financially after the star was arrested and stripped of his boxing licence for refusing to enlist in Vietnam — leading to him being frozen out of the ring from March 1967 until October 1970.

Once he returned to the ring, the money started flowing. Lonnie, his wife, handled Ali's business affairs as his health declined. Nick Woodhouse, the president of ABG, said: "He was the original global sports star — there was him and Pele. The Thrilla in Manila, the Rumble in the Jungle — he touched people everywhere at a time when sport was not a global business."

A plan has long been in place to handle publicity and commercial opportunities in relation to his death, Woodhouse said. "Without a doubt there will be increased commercial activity as there are so many fans who want a piece of that legacy."

KEEPING ALI IN MY SIGHTS

Photographer **Chris Smith** recalls assignments with 'one of the most recognisable faces on the planet'

Photographing great sporting events and personalities never fails to thrill. I've been doing it for more than 50 years and one of the highlights was photographing Muhammad Ali. Charisma, the power to charm and inspire, he had by the fistful, as well as magnetism to draw people to him. He was athletic, with great strength and speed. As he would be the first to point out, he had undoubted good looks. I first met him in 1964 at the famous Fifth Street Gym in Miami, when as Cassius Clay he was training for his first fight with the reigning world champion, Sonny Liston. After photographing his training session we piled into his Cadillac and headed across town for Liston's gym. When we arrived, Ali produced a steel bear trap from the back of the car and announced his intention to "use" it on Liston, who he described as a big ugly bear. Liston arrived for training to be greeted by a crowd of onlookers, at the centre of which was Ali screaming and brandishing the trap.

Liston looked at the alarming figure of Ali as though he was crazy. Most commentators agreed, believing that for the young Ali, getting into the ring with the fearsome Liston was a very bad idea. Ali had other ideas as he prepared for a fight which would announce the arrival of a force that would grip the world of sport like no other.

Another phenomenon in Miami at the same time was a group that would dominate pop music for years to come. The Beatles were in town as part of their first, hugely successful tour of the US. A sharp public relations mind had the idea of bringing them together with Ali to generate a maelstrom of publicity. The media had been alerted and the following day the gym was full to bursting as the Fab Four turned up to watch him train.

Ali, at the centre of the action with dozens of cameras and mikes trained on him, was in his element, declaiming to all and sundry. A media scrum can be a pretty hectic affair for a photographer: with not much time to be considered and reflective of what shots you're taking, you just pile in. The light in the gym was poor and as I was shooting with available light it was very tricky with so much action going on. I just shot whatever presented itself, not knowing for sure what I had got. The one certainty was that with all the activity in the poor light, a lot of the frames would have camera shake. So it proved, but you only need one shot if it's good enough. The resulting picture, although a slightly corny pose of Ali jabbing one Beatle with a chain reaction running through the group, had the merit of containing arguably the five most recognisable faces on the planet. I have a print on my wall today and the memory still brings a chuckle. A print of the meeting was auctioned for a children's charity and raised the remarkable sum of £12,000 — Ali never fails to attract.

I next saw Ali in 1971. His dispute with the US government over military service settled, he returned to the ring to fight Joe Frazier. With my great friend and colleague, Hugh McIlvanney, I went to the Fifth Street Gym to see Ali prepare for what was billed as the Fight of the Century.

Photographing Ali in the gym was always fascinating and I much prefer to shoot the training side of boxing, rather than the fight itself. So we would accompany Ali on his early-morning runs and hang out with him at the gym in the afternoons. The camera was always primed for use, the shutter speed and aperture constantly being adjusted as the light changed. I was looking for the shot that would give an insight into a world that went unseen by most. It's not always the shot with lots of action which does this, it can be a hand crossing Ali's face to wipe away sweat as the body beneath catches the light and shows his physical condition, or the moment of quiet reflection.

"Seeing" the picture and timing when you take it are critical, but when you get it right it is hugely satisfying. Hugh and I operated independently around the gym but when the words and pictures were produced, they always sat happily with each other. Two approaches to a single end.

His final fight in 1981 marked the end of an amazing career. The end of a journey that had captivated and thrilled the world and one which we all felt we had shared with the man they called The Greatest.

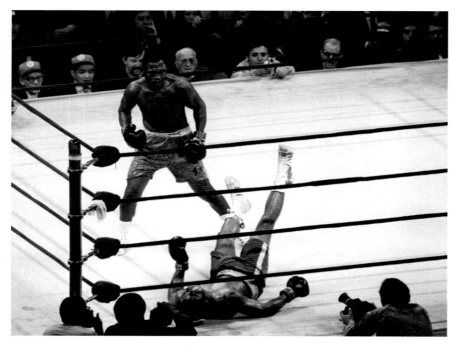

Left
Ali hits the canvas during his 1971 defeat at the hands of Joe Frazier

Right
Signs of strain during training at the Fifth Street Gym in Miami

Overleaf
George Harrison takes the hit as the Beatles clown with the fighter in 1964

Above
Ali liked to train in the relative peace of Deer Lake, Pennsylvania

Left
Drumming up publicity for his 1974 rematch with Frazier, which he won

Right
With daughter Hana and Veronica, his third wife, in New Orleans

Far right
Pictured in 1970 taking a breather at a gym session in Miami

IN DECLINE

1978-1984

Presidents get
assassinated, civil
rights leaders get
assassinated. The
world goes on.
I had my day.
You lose, you don't
shoot yourself

ALI WAS BEATEN FIVE TIMES, INCLUDING THIS
DEFEAT AGAINST LEON SPINKS, PICTURED RIGHT

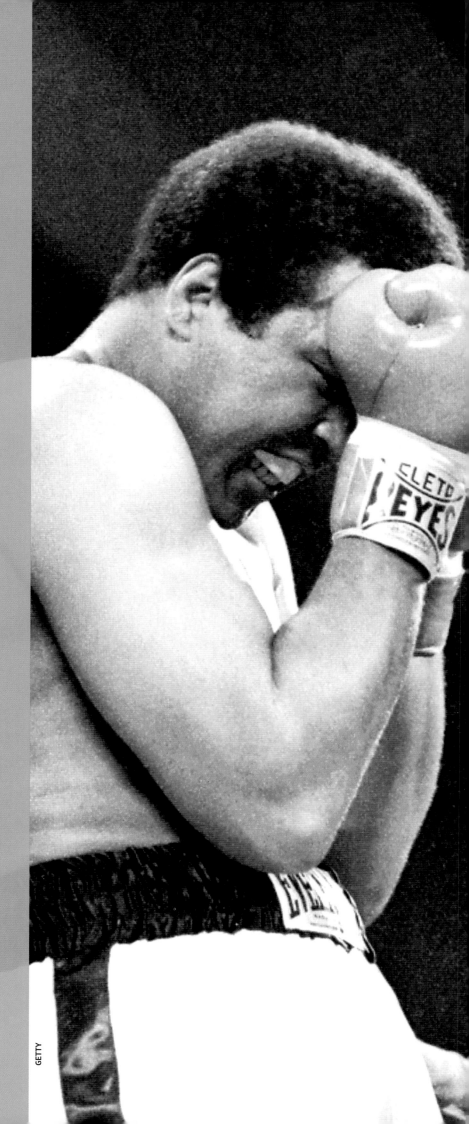

'I KNEW THE KING WAS GOING TO END UP A SHUFFLING WRECK'

The sad truth about Muhammad Ali is that he could have retired early and, without any trouble, lived the rest of his life as the king that he is. He could have avoided Parkinson's and the neurological damage he suffered. I could see all this coming and that was why I split with him and his camp in 1977, four years before his final retirement. I didn't want a part of it any more.

He should have got out after the "Thrilla in Manila" in 1975; that was the perfect full stop to a beautiful career. But his advisers and the boxing world thought: "Let's have some more." So we got to another Ken Norton fight — and every time he fought Norton he got killed. After that, they told me: "We're going to give him an easy fight and then he's going to retire." But the second fight after Norton was Earnie Shavers and Shavers could knock down a building. He was just so tough. I said: "That's not easy. You can't knock him out, so you've got 15 rounds of hell." Well, they didn't pay any attention to me and I left.

I stayed for Shavers, I knew I had to be there for that one, I knew I'd have a lot of work to do. I just wanted to get him through the fight and after Shavers I walked out. But I tried to make my point first. The Shavers fight was in New York and Ali's physical examination afterwards was so bad that the New York state doctor said: "If he goes back to New York, we're not going to license him any more." I got a copy of that letter plus the other physical evidence — there was blood in the urine, he was already neurologically damaged, he couldn't walk without shuffling a little bit, he was certainly mumbling and stumbling — and I went to him and to his managers. I wrote a letter to each of them and I listed his various injuries. I showed them where he was injured, why he was injured and what was going to happen to him. All that was in the letter, and they all ignored it.

Left

Trainer Angelo Dundee, far left, Dr Ferdie Pacheco and assistant trainer Drew Bundini Brown support Ali during his fight with Earnie Shavers in 1977

Muhammad Ali and his team did not heed the warnings about his health, according to the boxer's doctor **Ferdie Pacheco**

Ali and I were friends over it. He said: "I appreciate what you're saying." I said: "Ali, it's not fun any more, you are going to be a shambling wreck. Go to the gym and see these guys that talk funny — that's going to be you. You could save yourself now but you're not going to."

And he kept on going and like a crime, three years later, they put him in with Larry Holmes. They should have been arrested for malpractice. He suffered terribly in that fight. The end of his career was a disgrace to him and to his greatness. He's so great you can just about overlook it, but Ali couldn't get off. He liked it so much and the people who were sucking him dry for money couldn't stop the money train.

You see, once you get to the end, everything is wrong. Your body is no longer responding to the injuries, you're not elastic any more, you don't bounce back. If he had stopped after Manila, he wouldn't be the way he is now. After Shavers, he already had a lot of damage, but he may not have been as bad, even though he was already showing damage from prolonged fighting.

You don't stay in the sport without paying the price. A guy like Lennox Lewis should be cheered and made a hero. He got out with all his marbles and he walks out with his head held high. He's smart; the other guys aren't.

I know it's not proven that boxing gave Ali Parkinson's, but the fact is that neurological damage can follow the course of either Parkinson's or Alzheimer's. Repeated blows to the head end in neurological damage, that's an undeniable fact; what that damage is, what name you put on it, doesn't make any difference. You just ain't the same.

Ali handled his illness like the champion he was but he always told me: "You're the only one that was right."

Ferdie Pacheco, "the Fight Doctor," was Ali's physician and cornerman for 15 years before becoming a TV boxing analyst

FROM THE ARCHIVES

JOKING ALI KNOCKS HIS ILLNESS

TUNKU VARADARAJAN, THE TIMES, SEPTEMBER 10, 1997

Muhammad Ali, arguably the most popular sportsman this century, has given his most detailed account to date of the Parkinson's from which he suffers.

"I'm still the greatest," Ali, 55, told reporters in Chicago, his irresistible vanity undimmed by years of illness. Speaking at a press conference organised by Pharmacia & Upjohn, an American pharmaceuticals company, the former world heavyweight champion said there was no necessary link between the degenerative brain disorder and boxing. Whispering hoarsely, he added that "boxing's much tougher"

than the disease. Although Ali's slurred speech and jolting movements continue to break the hearts of those who once saw him float like a butterfly and sting like a bee, the occasion did at least show that "The Greatest" was in buoyant spirits.

His wife, Lonnie, was with him and together they appealed for a greater public awareness of the disease. Ali's condition, which affects more than 1.5million Americans, has led to a shuffling walk, frozen facial expression and shaking hands, all shown worldwide when he lit the flame at the Olympic Games in Atlanta last year.

Ali's wife said: "Muhammad has refused to let Parkinson's slow him down ... we are planning to build a gym where he will work out daily, hitting the bag and sparring."

She said he walked up to five miles a day, but Ali cheerfully disagreed with her, shaking his head and holding up all ten fingers. At the end of the meeting, Ali and his wife were given a pair of red boxing gloves.

Rising to his feet and arching his eyelids, he delivered a jab: "I come all the way here, give you a nice little talk, and this is all you give me?"

NEIL LEIFER

THE LAST BOUT

Defeat against Trevor Berbick was a shabby affair, writes **Hugh McIlvanney**

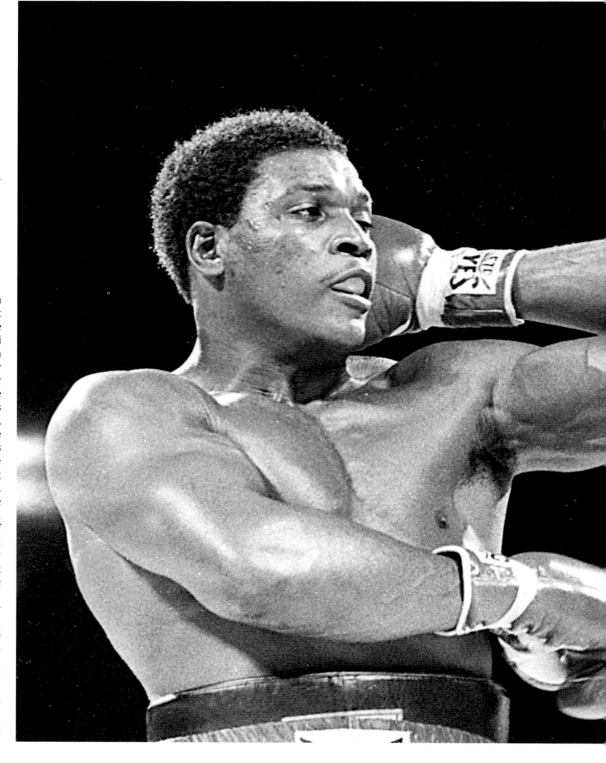

Graceful exits are rare in professional boxing but few great champions have gone out more miserably than Muhammad Ali in the Bahamas on Friday, when he lost on points to Trevor Berbick in a thoroughly inept fight that was the melancholy centrepiece of a shabby promotion. The most remarkable career the game has ever known was, we must earnestly hope, brought to its final close by a tinny rattle from the Bahamian cowbell that was dredged up from somewhere to impersonate the timekeeper's instrument the bungling organisers of the event neglected to provide. When the incongruous noise signalled the end of the 10th round Ali, who had been forced to acknowledge the full, sad cost of serving more than half of his 40 years in the prize ring as he laboured unsuccessfully to hide the decay of his reflexes, timing and athleticism, was well behind on the scorecards of all three judges.

Berbick is the kind of lumbering swinger he would have first embarrassed and then demolished in his prime but even the additional sluggishness imposed on the Jamaican's work by conspicuous idleness in his training could not save this pathetically diminished Ali.

To see him lose to such a moderate fighter in such a grubby context was like permanent exile on the back of a garbage truck. The one blessing was that he was steadily exhausted rather than violently hurt by the experience. Even that consolation was worryingly diluted when most of his inner circle, from his wife Veronica to his manager Herbert Muhammad to his recently acquired friend John Travolta, thrust distorted and dangerously reassuring interpretations of the fight into his head. "I don't want him to fight but you people are brainwashing him into thinking he did badly tonight," Veronica said in Ali's dressing room. She insisted her man had done more worthwhile punching than Berbick.

Above
Berbick won after 10 undistinguished rounds at the Queen Elizabeth Sports Centre in Nassau

"Father Time caught up with me," Ali said, so faintly only the two or three of us at the front of the crowding group of interviewers could make out the words. "I feel tired. Berbick was too strong, more aggressive. I just had the feeling I could do this thing. My mind said 'do it' but I know I didn't have it out there. I did good for a 39-year-old." Yesterday he indicated firmly that he will be steered towards retirement by the memory of how feebly he coped with Berbick, the realisation of how far he has declined from

the towering standards of the past. Once his speed and co-ordination deserted him, he was bound to look worse than ordinary because he did not have the remnants of an orthodox method to hide behind. At the Queen Elizabeth Sports Centre he was just an ageing, overweight ex-champion. What happened in the eighth was a tribute to the courage Ali will never lose. In that round he went up on his toes and bravely attempted to jab and dance, stick and move. Ali took the eighth but was soon settling heavily on

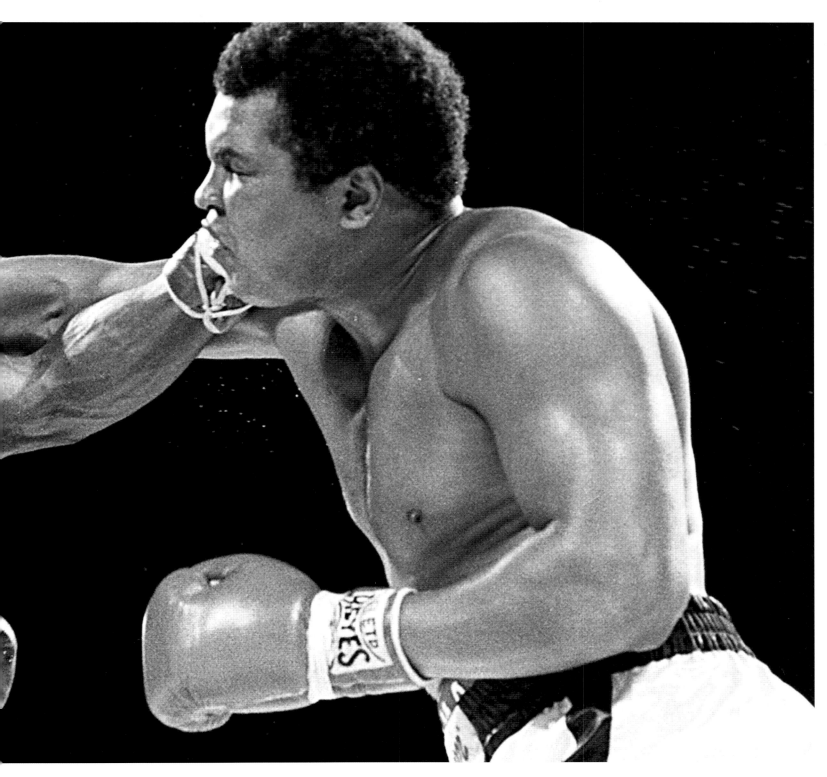

his heels again and when he was on the wrong end of the undistinguished doings in the ninth and 10th, there could be only one result.

The flavour of the occasion was not improved by the violence with which Ali's strong-arm battalion repelled pressmen and broadcasters who tried to follow the loser into his dressing room. Inside there was a contrasting tranquillity, especially when Ali's 11-year-old daughter from his previous marriage squirmed onto his knee to

Ali could not hide the decay of his reflexes, timing and athleticism

kiss his battered head. His mother squeezed through his interrogators to embrace him. "Good try, honey," she said and then to us: "I didn't cry. I'm not worried about his losing. I'm just glad he didn't get hurt." Angelo Dundee, who has run Ali's corner for 20 years, was also happy about that but one or two on the fringes of the entourage looked as if they suspected they were about to be hurt — by being deprived of regular swellings around the cash pocket. Everyone in that room was having thoughts about

how it would be when Ali had left this scene behind for ever.

A wire-service reporter was asking the fighter if, when he had quit, he would find time to talk President Gadaffi out of sending Libyan hit squads after President Reagan. With Muhammad Ali that is supposed to be a practical inquiry. As was said after that Roman heavyweight was done in, when comes such another?

Edited extract from McIlvanney on Boxing (Mainstream Publishing)

FINAL YEARS

1996-2016

The man who views the world at 50 the same as he did at 20 has wasted 30 years of his life

---

ALI REFLECTS IN AN INTERVIEW IN PLAYBOY MAGAZINE, NOVEMBER 1975

'OLYMPIC FLAME FAILS TO SHINE LIGHT ON INJUSTICE'

When Ali lit the Olympic flame in 1996 it was supposed to herald a new era for America, but as **Matthew Syed** reported in 2011, the reality proved to be very different

I shed a tear when Muhammad Ali lit the Olympic flame in Atlanta in 1996, and not just because I had failed to qualify for the Games by the tiniest of margins. I watched that extraordinary moment on television and found myself gripped, like millions of others around the world, by powerful and complex emotions.

This was about more than a former boxer holding a torch dipped in petroleum, more than mere choreography. This was a man who symbolized many of the deepest scars in postwar American history; a political subversive so wounded by the injustices of Jim Crow segregation that he threw away his Olympic gold medal; a man who had objected to the war in Vietnam even as support for the conflict was near its apotheosis.

In the moment of lighting, it was as if something changed. This was a moment not just of symbolism, but of atonement, of moving on, not just for a man, but for a nation and a world. The very selection of Ali was somehow an acknowledgement of past wrongs, a statement of remorse, as well as a powerful assertion of hope for the future. As one American newspaper put it: "It was a moment of collective healing".

Let us rewind to that Ali moment in Atlanta. It was powerful in terms of what it said about race relations, a 'moment of healing' as that American newspaper put it. But – and it is curious just how easy it is to forget this – nothing changed in the material condition of black Americans in that unforgettable moment of ignition.

In the moments after the flame was lit, blacks continued to earn 25 per cent less than whites. They continued to dominate the prison population and to make up the majority of the ghetto population. They continued to be less likely to be invited to a job interview (50 per cent less likely) even when holding precisely the same qualifications as whites. The iconography of the Olympics changed none of that; indeed, these inequities fester today.

Right

Ali holds the Olympic torch at Atlanta in 1996 but, for all the powerful emotions unleashed, little changed for black Americans

REX

ALI THE FAMILY MAN

Muhammad Ali had four wives and nine children during an at times tangled personal life. By **Jon Ungoed-Thomas**

From when he was only six months old, Muhammad Ali entranced those around him with his fast jab and flailing arms. His mother always said she was the victim of his first knockout punch when his whirring "muscle arms" caught her in the mouth, leading to the removal of her two front teeth.

The dizzying style and breakneck speed shattered boxing conventions and humbled opponents, but was also reflected in a tortuous and tangled personal life. He had four wives and nine children, including an adopted son.

In older age he lived in peace and often seclusion with his wife of nearly 30 years, Yolanda "Lonnie" Williams, but also travelled regularly. Williams had known him since she was a child and considered it a life mission to care for Ali and protect his legacy. "He is one of the rare individuals – like the late Mother Teresa and Princess Diana were – who can walk anywhere and be well received by millions," she said in 1992. "My role in life is to support and assist him to go forward and fulfil this mission. I was born a natural carer and Muhammad is the reason."

He was said to have relived his past glories by watching his fights. He suffered sporadic depression from Parkinson's, with which he was diagnosed in 1984.

There was also significant strife in Ali's

Above
Two of Ali's daughters, Maryum, left, and Hana, relax

extended family, with allegations that Williams had restricted family access to the former world champion and had too much control over his personal wealth. Three years ago Ali's brother, Rahman Ali, complained in an interview with the National Enquirer that the former boxer was a "prisoner in his own home".

"If my brother had his faculties I'd be living in a mansion because he always looked after me . . . When he dies no one will get anything – zero," he said.

Muhammad Ali Jr, the boxer's son, complained in 2014 that he was living off food stamps to survive in a rundown Chicago neighbourhood. He alleged Williams made it difficult for him to get access to his father.

Ali met his first wife Sonji Roi, a former cocktail waitress, in July 1964 and married her the following month. He was 22. The relationship with Roi buckled under Ali's devotion to Islam and she complained of being coerced into adopting Muslim dress and customs. "I wasn't going to take on all the Muslims," she said. "If I had, I probably

Above right
A man with a pram: Ali goes for a run with twin daughters Jamillah and Rasheda in 1971

would have ended up dead." The couple had no children and divorced in 1966.

The following year Ali married Belinda Boyd, who was 17. They had four children: Maryum, twins Jamillah and Rasheda, and Muhammad Ali Jr.

Boyd changed her name to Khalilah Ali and converted to Islam. She said later: "Even though he was eight years older than me, I was a little smarter than him and a little bit more educated too. And helping and guiding him was the best time of my life."

Ali was repeatedly unfaithful and left Boyd for the actress Veronica Porsche, who he had met in 1974 at the "Rumble in the Jungle" against George Foreman in Zaire where they had a secret "marriage" ceremony. They were legally married in 1977 and had two children, Hana and Laila, before divorcing in 1986.

Ali and Williams were married later that year, but had known each other since her family became neighbours of Ali's family in 1962. The couple adopted a child, Asaad Amin. Ali has two other children, Miya and Khaliah, from affairs.

Champion Laila proves a chip off the old block

Like father, like daughter. And this particular Ali stayed unbeaten during her time as a boxer
By **Brian Doogan**

The self-proclaimed Greatest is the most famous boxer of all. Sadly, by the time his daughter Laila decided to follow in his footsteps, Ali was in the grip of Parkinson's and was unable to exert the sort of influence on his daughter's career that he may have wanted to.

Laila made her debut in 1999 and proved she was a chip off the old block by knocking out April Fowler in the first round. Many boxing

Above
Laila Ali won all her 24 fights during a boxing career spanning eight years

fans wanted to see her in the ring with Freeda Foreman, George's daughter, or Joe Frazier's daughter, Jackie Frazier-Lyde. On the evening of June 8, 2001, Ali and Frazier-Lyde finally met, with Ali winning in eight rounds.

She won four world titles and finished her boxing career unbeaten in 24 contests, 21 by knockout and has since become a fitness expert and television personality.

THE WOMAN WHO CARED

Before his death
Karen Bartlett talked to
Lonnie, Muhammad
Ali's fourth wife and
lifelong friend

When Yolanda "Lonnie" Williams was six years old she looked out of her front door in Louisville, Kentucky, and saw an energetic young man holding court to a wide-eyed gaggle of neighbourhood boys, including her brother. "Who's that big man?" she asked her mother, not knowing that the answer would change her life.

"That's Cassius Clay," her mother told her. "The Champ", "The Louisville Lip", the 1960 Olympic gold medallist. Lonnie crossed the street to find out what all the fuss was about: "He was wearing a crisp white shirt and a black bow tie, and all the boys were crowding around trying to listen to him. He saw that I was the only girl and he beckoned me over and talked to me — but he scared me, he was so huge."

Despite her apprehension, it proved to be the start of a lifelong conversation. "Before we got married I knew Muhammad was famous," she says. "But he was also the guy across the street who came to our house and talked to me, and ate with me and my parents. It wasn't until after we got married, that I realised the enormity of his celebrity. We would go to Egypt and old women would come up to him crying and holding him like a son. In Pakistan, grown men would chase him through the airport. It was quite shocking."

She admits that the legacy of Muhammad Ali meant many things to people — and that Ali himself wasn't always so universally loved. Back in the days when he was Cassius Clay, living in a modest house across Grand Avenue from the Williams family, he played a more divisive role in American life by joining Nation of Islam and refusing the draft to join the Vietnam War.

"We never talked about race in our house. People were people and that was it," she says. Lonnie was a student at Vanderbilt University in Tennessee and later became a successful businesswoman: "If I've been discriminated against because of my colour or sex, I've never noticed it."

Always in the background of her life was

Right
Muhammad Ali catches up with kids in a neighbourhood near his parents' house in Louisville, Kentucky

UNTIL THE END

'He was my daddy but he was also daddy to the world'

Muhammad Ali's daughter Hana Ali tells **Beverley D'Silva** about the humble, generous side to her famous father

Above
Lonnie and Muhammad were childhood friends who married in 1986. 'He had the full package,' she says

Muhammad Ali. "When I was about 17 I had an epiphany that we would get married and be together," she says. "It was more of a moment of knowing your destiny, rather than lovesick yearning. Muhammad had other wives, and I liked them. I went out with other guys, and I even thought about becoming engaged to one." Ultimately, though, none could compare to Ali.

"He had the full package," she says. "He had the perfect human physique. Look at him not as a woman would look at a man, but artistically — he was beautiful. And he was so vivid and alive. He had this incredible confidence and self-assurance."

It was his Parkinson's diagnosis that brought them together. "Muhammad was always in my life. When I was a little girl he was sitting at the kitchen table telling me about the importance of the 'heart', telling me about life — looking back he was rehearsing speeches he gave to college students. I was like a little sister to him. So, later, when he called me after his third marriage broke down, I knew something was wrong, I could hear it in his voice. He knew something was wrong, too, he just wasn't himself."

Lonnie flew out to be with him, and encouraged him to see a doctor. After the diagnosis she stayed with him for support and their relationship "gradually evolved".

"Muhammad is not romantic. Any romance came and went with his first wife, Sonji. He didn't get down on bended knee. Our relationship was a natural progression, you knew it was going to happen."

The couple adopted a son, Asaad, now 25, and Lonnie became Muhammad's primary carer. "Having Parkinson's opened Muhammad up to more people. Before he was 'perfect', but by having this illness people saw that he is just like everyone else. It made him seem more accessible."

Above
Lonnie and Muhammad at a celebrity fight night in Phoenix, Arizona

He was so vivid and alive. He had this incredible confidence

Dad was a loving, sensitive, patient person, and while the world saw the hero, we got to see the humble side of him. But by the time I was four, I realised he wasn't all mine. Once, he was carrying me through an airport and we saw crowds telling him he was the greatest. I felt waves of love coming at him, and later he told me he was my daddy, but he was also daddy to the world. Dad was generous to a fault; he bought many homeless families to our house, he'd also book them into hotels and pay their bills. In 1981 he heard a man was threatening to jump off a building in the Beverly Wilshire hotel. He took me there with him, and he sat on the ledge talking to the guy until he came inside.

Below
Muhammad Ali, with his third wife Veronica, and their daughter Hana, arrive at Heathrow Airport in 1977

"All I did was stand up for what I believed."

Muhammad Ali.

1942-2016

LOVE #ALI

FAITH HOPE

Verses of the Koran echoed around the hall

Left
Boxing gloves and a message sit among flowers at a memorial at the Muhammad Ali Center

Right
Mourners try to get close to the funeral procession in Louisville, Kentucky

GETTY IMAGES/AP

A NATION UNITED IN GRIEF

Political and religious differences were put aside in tribute to Ali at what one American called 'a royal funeral' in the boxer's home town, **Will Pavia** reported from Louisville

Thousands of Americans lined up at the front of a vast grey hall in northern Kentucky at noon to bid farewell to their champion. "Allahu akbar!" they cried.

It was a prayer heard across the land.

The body of Muhammad Ali lay in a coffin before a black curtain in the Freedom Hall, a hangar-like building beside a fairground south of Louisville that was the crucible for Ali's early career. Now he lay here in a coffin, facing Mecca, in a service that was being watched across America.

"He is like a magnet that's drawing everybody," said Fatima Khan, 57, a chaplain from Chicago, who stood three rows from the front of the hall.

In a torrid election season, when Donald Trump has called for a ban on Muslim immigrants, the death of Ali presented America with its first national Muslim funeral. "It is building a consciousness for American Muslims," said Ms Khan, before the voice of an imam, singing verses of the Koran, echoed around the hall. "We have to define ourselves. This is one person who is bringing everyone together and establishing our identity. His inspiration gave hope to so many people that you can lift yourself up."

It was to be expected that the funeral of Ali would bring the country to a standstill. "It's basically a royal funeral," said Randy Webber, 54, president of the Smoketown Neighbourhood Association. The Louisville district is where Ali trained at a boxing gym run by a local police officer. "It's the biggest we have seen since Martin Luther King and Bobby Kennedy in 1968."

It was not immediately obvious, perhaps, that the funeral would place the faith of Islam at the centre of a moment of national mourning. He had joined the Nation of Islam at the height of his fame, and later converted to Sunni Islam, but the fact of his faith receded from the public consciousness as he withdrew from the public stage.

In a memoir written with his daughter Hana, Ali said he would like to have become "a Muslim Billy Graham" at the close of his boxing career, but his Parkinson's had prevented it. "God had a different plan for me," he wrote.

Yet those who knew Ali in his last decades said he still observed the tenets of his faith: the writer Davis Miller, visiting for Sunday lunch, told how Ali had vanished upstairs abruptly to pray.

AP/GETTY IMAGES

One of his last public statements was that "we as Muslims have to stand up to those who use Islam to advance their own personal agenda". Some interpreted it as a rebuke to Mr Trump, a long-time friend, who had just called for a "total and complete shutdown of Muslims entering the United States".

Bob Gunnell, Ali's spokesman, insisted that it was not aimed at Mr Trump specifically. The billionaire is believed to have inquired whether he could attend yesterday's service. "He would be welcome," Mr Gunnell told reporters. He said Ali specifically wanted the service to be inclusive.

It took the form of a jenazah, a traditional ceremony of prayers which prepare the deceased for burial. Members of Ali's family, old neighbours and friends, and leading figures from the different worlds in which he once bobbed and weaved duly trooped into the Freedom Hall yesterday morning. There was the Reverend Jesse Jackson, decrying to a crowd the anti-Muslim rhetoric heard in this election season; there was the boxing promoter Don King, arriving with an entourage, suited, his grey hair a little shorter than it once was, a scarf in

Above
Mike Tyson, left, Lennox Lewis, second left, and Will Smith, right, applaud during the memorial service

the colours of the American flag wrapped around his neck.

Eddie Mustafa Muhammad, 64, a former heavyweight, had come from Las Vegas. "Ali means everything to me," he said. "We boxed many times together." Ali was then at the end of his career but he still moved like lightning, he added. "He helped me to become a world champion." He repeated, with awe, a story told by one of Ali's daughters: that the heart of the man who first made his mark on the world as Cassius Clay had continued to beat for 30 minutes after all his other organs failed. "Look at the way he went out," he said.

Wallace Dean Muhammad II, whose grandfather, Elijah Muhammad, led the Nation of Islam and was a mentor to Ali, arrived surrounded by a phalanx of men in suits. He said the fiery, separatist rhetoric of his grandfather had helped Ali to craft a black identity and given him the strength to make his stand against the draft during the Vietnam War. "It was shock therapy treatment," he said. "If it wasn't for Elijah Muhammad, I don't know if Ali would have fought the way he did."

The event seemed a strange medley of

American culture. In the fairground beside the hall, a rollercoaster ascended a steep track and people swung on chairs beneath a carousel. A man in a white cowboy hat stood in the road, holding the reins of a horse. On its back was a white robe, boxing gloves and shoes. "It represents the soldier who is taking his last ride," said Jerry Martin, 54, an air force veteran from Virginia. "The boots are facing backwards because he is saying goodbye. It is something they did for George Washington and for Kennedy."

A large party of Bangladeshi Americans, who had driven from Chicago, stood outside the hall. Mohammed Mortoja, 47, a computer programmer, remembered the day 20 years ago when he won the visa lottery and the right to come to the US. "America had a very positive image throughout the Muslim world. After all these wars happening, that has changed," he said.

And now there is Donald Trump.

Mr Mortoja hoped the sight of an American hero being buried as a Muslim might restore the old image of America. "Equal rights, freedom of religion — this is the dream for all of us," he said. "For all of the world."

Above
Wife Lonnie and Muhammad Ali's daughter Laila attend an Islamic Muslim service on June 9. Laila is holding her daughter Sydney

Left
Rahman Ali speaks of his brother's legacy at the museum of the Ali childhood home

REMEMBERING THE CHAMP

'Our hearts are literally hurting. But we are so happy daddy is free now' – Hana Ali, his daughter

'Muhammad Ali shook up the world. And the world is better for it. We are all better for it' – President Barack Obama

'Muhammad Ali was one of the greatest human beings I have ever met. No doubt he was one of the best people to have lived in this day and age' – George Foreman

'If Muhammad didn't like the rules, he rewrote them' – Lonnie, Ali's widow

'Athlete, civil rights leader, humanitarian, man of faith. Rest in peace' – Australian prime minister Malcolm Turnbull

'God came for his champion. So long great one #TheGreatest #RIP' – Mike Tyson

'What I most admired him for was his refusal to compromise on his belief and value system' – Imran Khan, Pakistan cricketer and politician

'Ali will never die. Like Martin Luther King his spirit will live on. He stood for the world' – fight promoter Don King

' The world has lost a truly great man' – Sir Paul McCartney

THE COMPLETE RECORD

He started his professional career as Cassius Clay, a raw but promising talent, and hung up his gloves 21 years later as Muhammad Ali, The Greatest. By **Ron Lewis**

🏆 World title fight

1960

1 *Oct 29*
Tunney Hunsaker
Louisville Won on Points Round 6
Just 54 days after winning Olympic gold, the 18-year-old Cassius Clay won every round against Hunsaker, a West Virginia police chief, who lasted the distance despite being cut.

2 *Dec 27*
Herb Siler
Miami Beach W Ref Stopped Contest 4
Clay's first bout with Angelo Dundee in his corner (he was there for 59 of 61 fights), was one-sided. The brave Siler kept swinging until the referee stopped the bout with him reeling against the ropes.

1961

3 *Jan 17*
Tony Esperti
Miami Beach W RSC 3
Clay's third win came on his 19th birthday against the totally overmatched "Big Tony" Esperti, who was jailed for life for murdering a mobster in 1967.

4 *Feb 7*
Jim Robinson
Miami Beach W Knockout 1
Robinson was a late sub for Willie Gullatt and a blown-up middleweight. He lasted just 93 seconds.

5 *Feb 21*
Donnie Fleeman
Miami Beach W Retired 6
Fleeman was a big step up in class, having beaten an over-the-hill Ezzard Charles, a former world champion. But he was no match for Clay and quit with a broken rib.

6 *Apr 19*
LaMar Clark
Louisville W KO 2
Clark had a world record 44 successive knockout wins, but was outclassed by Clay, who predicted the winning round for the first time and landed a four-punch knockout combination.

7 *Jun 26*
Duke Sabedong
Las Vegas W Points 10
Sabedong, a 6ft 6in Hawaiian, towered

over his opponent and resorted to fouling after Clay began taunting him.

⑧ Jul 22
Alonzo Johnson
Louisville W Points 10
Clay produced a sluggish display and was booed by fans, but won by scores of 50-44, 48-45 and 48-47.

⑨ Oct 7
Alex Miteff
Louisville W RSC 6
His first foreign opponent, Miteff, from Argentina, took the fight to Clay in the early rounds before being battered to the canvas in the sixth.

⑩ Nov 29
Willi Besmanoff
Louisville W RSC 7
Besmanoff, a German who survived a brief incarceration at Buchenwald concentration camp, where he was sent because his father was a Jew, was another boxer whose bravery was not matched by his skills. He folded in the seventh round.

1962
⑪ Feb 19
Sonny Banks
New York W RSC 4
Banks is remembered as the first man to knock down the future champion. Clay was on top when Banks landed a left hook that dropped Clay on to his backside. It was only a blip, though, as Clay fulfilled his prediction of winning in four.

⑫ Mar 28
Don Warner
Miami Beach W RSC 4
Clay's win over Warner was not straightforward, either, as he was rocked by a right at the end of the third round.

Left page
Archie Moore, a former world champion at light-heavyweight, was 45 years old but still fancied his chances in 1962. He was beaten in four rounds

Left
Alex Miteff, in 1961, was Cassius Clay's first non-American opponent. The Argentinian started well but lost in the sixth

Right
A sellout crowd at Madison Square Garden in 1963 saw Doug Jones give a good account before losing on points

He responded in the next round by hitting Warner straight through the ropes.

⑬ Apr 23
George Logan
Los Angeles W RSC 4
Logan, a potato farmer from Idaho, suffered a broken nose and cuts as he was ground down by Clay in four rounds.

⑭ May 19
Billy Daniels
New York W RSC 7
Daniels was unbeaten but did not have the skills to hold off Clay, as a bad cut brought an end to the increasingly one-sided action in the seventh round.

⑮ Jul 20
Alejandro Lavorante
Los Angeles W RSC 5
Lavorante, from Argentina, was seen as Clay's first big test. He was rated a top prospect after knocking out Zora Folley, a future Ali opponent. It excited the fans too, with 11,000 cramming into the Los Angeles Sports Arena. Lavorante was saved by the bell in the second and knocked down twice in the fifth.

⑯ Nov 15
Archie Moore
Los Angeles W RSC 4
Moore, the "Old Mongoose", had been a long-reigning world light-heavyweight champion before moving up to heavyweight. Now 45, he could still talk a good fight and knew Clay well, the young

fighter having been in his camp for his professional debut. "The only way I'll fall in four is tripping over Clay's prostrate frame," Moore said after being told of Clay's prediction. But the old champion could not cope with Clay's speed and was knocked down three times.

1963
⑰ Jan 24
Charlie Powell
Pittsburgh W KO 3
Powell had played basketball, American football and baseball as well as boxing professionally. His efforts were used up trying to chase Clay and land one big punch. Clay finished him off with a three-punch combination in the third round.

⑱ Mar 13
Doug Jones
New York W Points 10
Madison Square Garden was sold out for a classic fight, with Jones not only lasting the distance but, in the eyes of many, doing enough to win. Clay took a unanimous decision – by a landslide in the eyes of Joe LoScalzo, the referee, and by just a round for the two ringside judges.

⑲ Jun 18
Henry Cooper
Wembley Stadium, London W RSC 5
One of the most famous nights in British sport, as the home hero came close to

Ali's arm is held aloft after he pummelled Brian London to defeat at Earls Court in August, 1966. A few months earlier he had beaten Henry Cooper, also in London

upsetting the young pretender. A left hook in the fourth round dropped Clay into the ropes and onto the floor. The bell sounded almost instantly to give Clay a needed break, which Dundee tried to extend by claiming his man's glove was torn. It got him a few extra seconds, and he ensured Cooper, who was badly cut over the left eye, would not get another chance. Clay landed punch after punch, the blood flowed and the referee stopped it.

1964

Feb 25
Sonny Liston

Miami Beach W Retired 7
The night Clay shook up the world. Largely written off against a highly regarded champion, Clay made Liston look slow. He took the title when Liston, claiming an injured shoulder, refused to come out for the seventh round. A week later, Clay became Muhammad Ali.

1965

May 25
Sonny Liston

Lewiston, Maine W KO 1
One of the most infamous fights in heavyweight history took place in front of just 2,412 fans after many cities showed no interest because of Ali's new affiliation to the Nation of Islam, and his name change. A quick right dropped Liston and Ali stood over him telling him to get up. He did, eventually, and the referee, Jersey Joe Walcott, waved the fight on, before Nat Fleischer, editor of The Ring magazine, shouted that Liston had been counted out. Rumours persist that Liston took a dive.

Nov 22
Floyd Patterson

Las Vegas W RSC 12
Ali did nothing to boost his public image

by taunting the popular two-time world champion even during the fight, calling Patterson an "Uncle Tom" who was boxing for "White America". Ali toyed with the former champion before the stoppage.

1966

Mar 29
George Chuvalo

Toronto W Points 15
In 1966, Ali refused the US draft, which led to a planned defence against Ernie Terrell in Chicago being declared "illegal" by the state of Illinois. Instead he faced Chuvalo, who forced Ali to fight every step of the way.

May 21
Henry Cooper

Highbury, London W RSC 6
With Wembley booked for the World

Cup, Cooper got his chance at revenge at Highbury, with 46,000 watching. This time there was no knockdown, as Ali stayed out of trouble and banged away with straight punches until another vicious cut opened up above Cooper's left eye and forced a sixth-round stoppage.

Aug 6
Brian London

Earls Court, London W KO 3
While many had believed that Cooper could beat Ali, few gave London a chance. For two rounds Ali played with him before unloading a fierce barrage in the third that dropped London for the full count.

Sep 10
Karl Mildenberger

Frankfurt, Germany W RSC 12
Ali was never completely at ease with Mildenberger's southpaw style. The

German was brave, taking plenty of punishment and being floored twice before he was stopped in the 12th.

㉗ Nov 14
Cleveland Williams
Houston W RSC 3
The outclassed challenger was down four times before he was put out of his misery.

1967

㉘ Feb 6
Ernie Terrell
Houston W Points 15
Ali showed his vicious side as he dished up a 15-round beating to Terrell, who had made the mistake of not acknowledging his new name. Early on, the 6ft 6in challenger had some success as he used his reach advantage, but by the seventh round he was cut, hurt and heading for

Above
British challenger Richard Dunn on his way to defeat in Munich in 1976. Dunn was dropped five times and did well to last five rounds

defeat. Instead of going for the finish, though, Ali backed off and taunted Terrell, saying: "What's my name?" The beating continued to the end.

㉙ Mar 22
Zora Folley
New York W KO 7
In what would be his final fight for three and a half years, Ali was just about at his peak as he dismantled Folley, knocking him down in the fourth round and dropping him face-first in the seventh.

1970

㉚ Oct 26
Jerry Quarry
Atlanta W RSC 3
After so long away, Ali did not take long to get back into his groove, watched by a sellout crowd of 5,100 at Atlanta's City

Auditorium. A cut over Quarry's left eye brought a premature end to the action.

㉛ Dec 7
Oscar Bonavena
New York W RSC 15
Tough, crude and something of a wild man, Bonavena, from Argentina, went into the fight with the distinction of having become the first man to knock down Joe Frazier, the new champion, although he lost a split points decision to him. It took Ali time to subdue Bonavena, but he dropped him three times.

1971

㉜ Mar 8
Joe Frazier
New York L Points 15
It was billed as the Fight of the Century. Frazier, the unbeaten champion, faced Ali, the unbeaten former champion. For the first time, Ali struggled to deal with a pressure fighter and he was knocked down by a left hook in the last round on the way to losing a unanimous points decision.

㉝ July 26
Jimmy Ellis
Houston W RSC 12
Ellis, the former WBA champion, was one of Ali's best friends and a training partner. Angelo Dundee trained both and worked Ellis' corner. Ellis began well, but Ali rocked him in the fourth and was in control thereafter. In the 12th round, Ali stepped back and the referee stopped it.

㉞ Nov 17
Buster Mathis
Houston W Points 12
Injury had prevented Mathis going to the 1964 Olympics, where Frazier, his replacement, won gold. Ali played safe against his bigger opponent, but Mathis was soundly beaten.

㉟ Dec 26
Jurgen Blin
Zurich W KO 7
Blin, a German, was aggressive and horribly outclassed. A right uppercut and a big right cross floored him.

1972

㊱ Apr 1
Mac Foster
Tokyo W PTS 15
Ali's world tour continued with a dominant points win over Foster, an outclassed Vietnam War veteran.

㊲ May 1
George Chuvalo
Vancouver W PTS 12
A rematch resulted in more of the same as Ali pounded out an easy points victory against the Canadian.

38 *Jun 29*
Jerry Quarry
Las Vegas W RSC 7
A one-sided rematch. Quarry could not cope with Ali's speed and accuracy and, after Ali had built a huge lead, he stepped up the pace to force a stoppage.

39 *Jul 19*
Al Lewis
Croke Park, Dublin W RSC 11
Lewis was a former sparring partner of Ali's and was heavily knocked down for what seemed a long count in the fifth round, before Ali eased off.

40 *Sep 20*
Floyd Patterson
New York W RSC 7
Seven years after their first meeting Patterson, 37, convinced many that revenge was in order, but he was slowly busted up before being stopped.

41 *Nov 21*
Bob Foster
Stateline, Nevada W KO 8
Foster, a great light-heavyweight who had beaten Ali as an amateur, was too small to box full heavyweights. Ali knocked him down seven times.

1973
42 *Feb 14*
Joe Bugner
Las Vegas W Points 12
Bugner, the former British champion, was too cautious, and was also cut in the first round. Ali won easily.

43 *Mar 31*
Ken Norton
San Diego L Points 12
Few expected Norton to cause problems for Ali, but the former Marine broke Ali's jaw in the first round and outlasted him, winning a split decision.

44 *Sep 10*
Ken Norton
Los Angeles W Points 12
Ali was in better shape for the rematch and built an early lead before Norton rallied. This time Ali pulled it out in the last round to take a split decision.

45 *Oct 20*
Rudi Lubbers
Jakarta, Indonesia W Points 12
One of Ali's duller fights. He easily beat his Dutch rival after 12 uneventful rounds.

1974
46 *Jan 28*
Joe Frazier
New York W Points 12
Tactically, Ali got things right for this rematch, even if it was the poorest of their

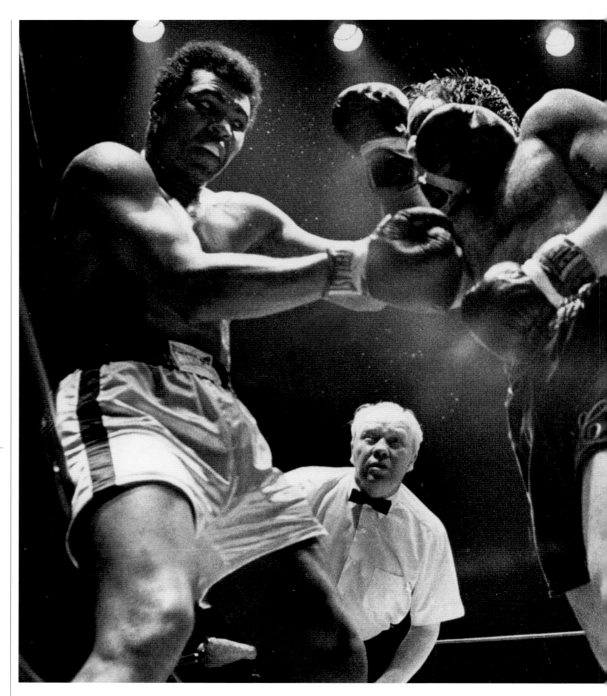

Above
George Chuvalo took a battering in Vancouver in 1972 but refused to drop. He was never knocked down in 93 fights

three meetings. He did plenty of holding in the ring. There had been spice in the build-up, the pair brawling in a TV studio.

47 *Oct 30*
George Foreman
Kinshasa, Zaire W KO 8
The Rumble In The Jungle was the fight that ensured Ali's greatness. Foreman threw everything at Ali from the opening bell and punched himself out before Ali struck to reclaim the title at 34.

1975
48 *Mar 24*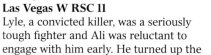
Chuck Wepner
Cleveland W RSC 15
Wepner gave Ali an unexpectedly tough

night and downed him with a right to the body in the ninth. Ali finally let loose in the final round and forced the stoppage.

49 *May 16*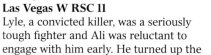
Ron Lyle
Las Vegas W RSC 11
Lyle, a convicted killer, was a seriously tough fighter and Ali was reluctant to engage with him early. He turned up the pace in the 11th.

50 *Jun 30*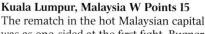
Joe Bugner
Kuala Lumpur, Malaysia W Points 15
The rematch in the hot Malaysian capital was as one-sided at the first fight, Bugner showing Ali too much respect and accepting defeat too early.

Oct 1
Joe Frazier

Manila, Philippines W Retired 14
The Thrilla in Manila was perhaps the most vicious fight in heavyweight history. Both men were well past their peak but Frazier in particular was driven by a great desire for revenge. They went toe-to-toe in sweltering heat, neither powerful enough to finish off the other. "It was like death," said Ali. "Closest thing to dyin' that I know of."

1976

 Feb 20
Jean-Pierre Coopman

San Juan, Puerto Rico W KO 5
After such a tough battle with Frazier, Coopman was little more than an exhibition for Ali, who knocked out the Belgian with a blistering combination.

Apr 30
Jimmy Young

Landover, Maryland W Points 15
Young was an up-and-coming challenger who had earned his ranking with a win over Ron Lyle. A sign that Ali was on the slide was that he weighed the heaviest of his career to date, 16st 6lb. Young frustrated Ali and after the champion tired, Young celebrated, believing he had won. Instead it was a unanimous points decision for Ali, which led to boos from the crowd.

 May 24
Richard Dunn

Munich W RSC 5
Ali was supposed to face Bernd August, but when Dunn pulled off a shock by beating the German for the European title seven weeks earlier, the Yorkshireman took his place. He was outclassed and knew it as much as everyone else. Ali floored him five times.

Sep 28
Ken Norton

New York W Points 15
Ali should have been retired by now but the money and the demands of those around him kept pushing him on. He was paid $6m to face his old rival Norton at Yankee Stadium on a wild night when the police went on strike, leaving the crowd in the Bronx at the mercy of muggers and gangs. Many believe Norton was robbed as well that night: Ali sneaked home by scores (in rounds) of 8-6 and 8-7 (twice).

1977

 May 16
Alfredo Evangelista

Landover, Maryland W Points 15
Evangelista, from Uruguay, was 13 years younger than Ali at 22, but he provided next to no threat. Ali resorted to leaning on the ropes for much of the fight before winning a unanimous decision.

 **Sep 29**
Earnie Shavers

New York W Points 15
Shavers was a famed heavy hitter, but Ali still had plenty of guile and stayed out of the way of Shavers' right hand until the final round, when he was rocked by a big right cross. Ali soon found his senses and had Shavers hanging on at the end.

1978

Feb 15
Leon Spinks

Las Vegas L Points 15
Spinks had won the Olympic light-heavyweight title and boxed just seven times as a professional (drawing one). Ali underestimated him and looked out of shape as the young challenger chased after him, battering him around the ring at times to win a split points decision.

 Aug 15
Leon Spinks

New Orleans W Points 15
A 63,350 crowd turned up at the Superdome for the rematch. This time Ali was in great shape; Spinks spent much of the previous six months partying. Ali won a unanimous points decision to become world heavyweight champion for a third time before announcing his retirement.

1980

Oct 2
Larry Holmes

Las Vegas L Retired 10
But it was not quite all over. A purse of $8m tempted Ali to face Larry Holmes, who had beaten Norton for the WBC title. It was a horrible sight. Holmes was at the peak of his powers while Ali was washed up, and had taken thyroid medication to slim down. Ali was Holmes' hero and by the end he was reluctant to continue hitting him before Angelo Dundee pulled out Ali at the end of the 10th round.

1981

Dec 11
Trevor Berbick

Nassau, Bahamas L Points 10
There was one last fight, in a field in the Bahamas, a bout that might have been called off until the very last minute. Ali could not cope with Berbick and was reduced to trying to paw out a slow jab before losing a unanimous points decision.

Overall record	
Bouts	61
Won	56
Lost	5

AL1
BY NUMB3RS

13

Different countries he boxed in as a professional: the United States, UK, Canada, Germany, Switzerland, Japan, Ireland, Indonesia, Zaire, Malaysia, the Philippines, Puerto Rico, the Bahamas

1

Albums he recorded

3

Times he won the world heavyweight title

3

Bouts in London — he boxed Henry Cooper at Wembley Stadium in 1963, then defended his world heavyweight title against Cooper at Highbury and Brian London at Earls Court, both in 1966

3

Left hooks, from Sonny Banks, Cooper and Joe Frazier, that knocked down Ali. He was also knocked down by a Chuck Wepner body shot

4,9

Marriages, children

5

Defeats as a professional

22

Age when he won the world heavyweight title. He was the youngest fighter to do so at the time

25

World title bouts Ali boxed in. He won 22 of them

39

Age in last contest, against Trevor Berbick in 1981

61

Knockout percentage as a professional in 548 rounds

10,000

Dollars for his first contract in 1960

8M

Dollars Ali was contracted to receive for his title fight against Larry Holmes in 1980